Path of the Hunter

Entering and Excelling in the Field of Criminal Investigation

LARRY F. JETMORE, Ph.D

D1519155

Looseleaf
Law Publications, Inc.

43-08 162nd Street • Flushing, NY 11358
www.LooseleafLaw.com • 800-647-5547

ISBN 1-932777-40-7

13-digit ISBN 978-1-93277-40-6

Library of Congress Cataloging-in-Publication Data

Jetmore, Larry F.
Path of the hunter : entering and excelling in the
field of criminal investigation / Larry F. Jetmore.
    p. cm.
ISBN-13: 978-1-932777-40-6 (pbk.)
ISBN-10: 1-932777-40-7 (pbk.)
1. Criminal investigation--United States. 2. Detectives--United States. 3. Criminal investigation--Vocational guidance--United States. 4. Detectives--United States--Examinations, questions, etc. 5. Police--United States--Examinations, questions, etc.
I. Title.
HV8073.J48 2007
363.25023'73--dc22

2007013869

Cover design by *Sans Serif, Inc., Saline, Michigan*

Table of Contents

Introduction

The primary purpose of this book is to provide students, law enforcement officers and others in investigative positions fundamental and advanced criminal investigation techniques. The investigative processes described in these pages offer utility in conducting any criminal investigation, regardless of whether it's a routine minor assault or a complex outdoor crime scene involving skeletal remains uncovered after having been buried for many years.

A secondary goal of this book is to provide individuals seeking advancement to detective or an investigative position in their agency with a methodology to achieve high scores in testing for promotion. Regardless of whether you'll be taking a written examination, an oral test, or going through an assessment center testing process, this book will sharpen your test-taking skills and provide you with a competitive edge in the promotional process. Even experienced investigators who want to improve their skills will find that the test prep section complements material on the investigative process.

This book operates on a basic premise—that the police do not work for, nor should they be supervised by, the judicial branch of government, i.e. prosecutors, state attorneys general, district attorneys, etc. As any grade school student should know, the police are part of the executive branch of government. The framers of our constitution believed in a balance of power among the legislative, executive, and judicial branches of government. In a democracy, the police don't prosecute or sentence individuals. We are meant to be independent from influence, and we take an oath to protect the innocent. We are neither for nor against prosecution. Simply put, investigators use the scientific method of inquiry to determine what happened and who is responsible. The evidence gathered then speaks for itself.

Before the twenty- or twenty-five-year retirement packages available to today's law enforcement officers, it wasn't unusual for police officers to stay on the job well into their sixties. On my first day as a detective I was partnered with a detective who was sixty-eight years old and had been investigating murders since I was in grade school. I thought I knew a lot about conducting investigations. All police officers are investigators, and I had spent years in patrol responding to every type of crime.

Our first day together as partners was not as I had imagined. These old-timers are a tough breed. You know the type: large beak nose, eyebrows as thick as windshield wipers, puffs of hair growing from the ears and nose, huge bushy mustache, wrists twice the normal size, ill-fitting suit, etc. Other than a few grunts, my new partner had little to say. We had been driving around the city for hours (he drove, of course), and when I finally gathered up the courage to initiate a conversation, the best I could come up with was, "So, exactly what is it that we do?"

Such a long time went by that I didn't think he heard me. Finally he looked over at me and with a kind of gruesome grin said, "We speak for the dead, kid. That's what we do. If you keep your mouth shut and your ears and eyes open, you might learn something."

So that's what this book is about. I was taught by a series of magnificent, talented people, and I want to pass on some of what they taught me. Although there is no substitute for experience, and I can't replicate through written communication the methods used by my mentors to teach me, I can show you the doorway and push you toward it.

Semper Fidelis,

Larry "The Jet" Jetmore

INVESTIGATING CRIMINAL BEHAVIOR

Chapter One

The Legal Process

Criminal Investigation Defined

I have a collection of books about criminal investigation that dates back some thirty years. One defines criminal investigation as *"the process of discovering, collecting, preparing, identifying and presenting evidence to determine what happened and who is responsible."*[1] Another defines it by merely stating a series of objectives, and a third offers that criminal investigation is *"the collection of information and evidence for identifying, apprehending and convicting suspected offenders"—a method of reconstructing the past.*[2]

All three definitions are legitimate, but no more than what we learned in the police academy—that an investigation seeks to determine the who, what, when, where, why, and how of something that happened or which we have a reasonable belief (hypothesis based on probability) is going to happen. To provide meaning to these definitions, it's critical to have a basic knowledge of criminal law.

The Investigative Process in a Democracy

In a democracy, the police are constrained by a formidable legal framework under which they are required to operate in order to determine whether a crime was committed and if so, who did it. Our Constitution, the Bill of Rights, and a host of legal interpretations by federal and state courts place limits on the methodology and practices used by the police in serving and protecting our people. Basic to the investigative process is that those who practice it must have an excellent understanding of not just the law, but how it must legally be applied.

This first chapter begins to outline the legal perspective of criminal investigation by defining terms and providing examples. Unless you work within this framework, be prepared to see the predators you have strived so hard to identify and lock up get away with their crimes because *you* didn't take the time to become skilled in the legal aspects of criminal investigation.

Crime

From a *sociological perspective,* crime is defined as anything a society says is a crime and for which it punishes transgressors. This global definition acknowledges that some degree of deviance is normal when you deal with large numbers (millions) of people, and that it's only when behavior becomes so deviant that it's recognized to be harmful to society and therefore must be sanctioned in some way that it is a crime.[3] Thus, *public harm* is a crime with one set of legal and evidentiary rules, and *private harm* is a tort (civil law) governed by another set of legal and evidentiary rules.

These differentiations are complicated even further by different definitions among the various states and jurisdictions relative to what is and is not criminal. For example, a sixteen-year-old male having consensual sexual intercourse with a fifteen-year-old female is criminal in many states because a fifteen-year-old is considered a child and therefore incapable of giving consent. In other states, the age of consent may be higher or lower, and if consensual sex is committed in those states, it might not be criminal. Because many Supreme Court decisions (*Miranda v. Arizona,* for example) deal with "knowing and intelligent" consent in asserting or giving up individual rights protected under the Constitution, it is basic to criminal investigation that we determine whether or not a crime has in fact been committed.

Further muddying the waters is that behavior (or lack of it) may be both a criminal and a civil matter. An example is a drunk driver who strikes a van from behind, killing several people. The driver might be charged by the police with negligent homicide with a motor vehicle (criminal law), and a civil suit (tort), might also be filed by surviving victims or the estate of the deceased in civil court seeking compensation. Note that in criminal court, the complainant or the one bringing charges against the defendant, is always the state, which indicates that the crime has been committed against all of the citizens of the state. You may have been the victim of a robbery, for example, but according to our laws, there is an assumption that criminal acts injure all of us, not just the individual. Because it's a crime against the state, technically there is no such thing as "dropping charges," although it may be difficult to prosecute a case if the victim, even under subpoena, refuses to testify. In contrast, in civil court, the case would be listed as *Johnson v. Smith,* indicating that a "private wrong" is being adjudicated.

There are many other definition of a crime. Under statutory law, a crime might be defined as "an act in violation of statutory law" (law passed by the state legislature) or "an act in violation of federal law" (a law passed by the U.S. Congress).

In most states, crimes are further defined and/or classified as being **felonies, misdemeanors** or **violations**. Deviant behavior that society considers to be very harmful is a felony; less harmful are misdemeanors; and the least harmful to society are violations that often result only in a fine—such as a motorist going through a stop sign. A felony is punishable by death or greater than a year in prison plus a fine. A misdemeanor is punishable by imprisonment of less than three hundred sixty-five days and/or a fine. A violation is punishable by a fine and, in some cases, imprisonment. Because definitions of crime and resulting punishment vary depending on whether they occur at the federal, state or local level, investigators must be experts in the criminal law within their jurisdictions.

Another basic premise in criminal law is that of **corpus delicti**—establishing evidence that a criminal act has in fact occurred. Suppose, for example, that after a heavy rainstorm, some hunters come across a burial mound in the deep woods with a skeletal hand sticking up from the ground. The body is so putrefied that hardly anything is left but a skeleton. After the crime scene is processed, it's found that there is no evidence at the scene (bullet casing, a hole through the skull, blunt force trauma to bones, etc.) to indicate that an unnatural death occurred. If the medical examiner who performs the autopsy can't determine whether the person died as a result of an unnatural death, do you have a crime? What would you charge a person with?

Closely related to *corpus delicti* are **elements of the crime.** These are specific factors that must occur for an act to be considered a type of crime. In most states, for an offense to be a robbery, there must be (1) a larceny (theft)—which has its own definition—by (2) force or threat of force. If the investigation can't prove each element of the crime, the case cannot proceed.

In addition, many types of crime have **criminal intent** or **mens rea** (Latin for "guilty mind") as an element of the crime. Criminal intent is often defined as "knowing an act to be illegal" or an "awareness of right from wrong," and with that awareness, a person chooses to violate the law, which can be problematic in some cases. The degree to which a person may be held criminally liable is often dependent on the person's mental state when the act was committed. For example, if an eight-year-old boy opens his grandfather's gun cabinet, takes out a loaded revolver and, in a game of cops and robbers, shoots his seven-year-old brother to death, has a crime been committed by the eight-year-old child? Is the child capable of forming criminal intent?

The Constitution and the Bill of Rights

Our forefathers were fearful of strong central government. In 1789, two years after the signing of the Constitution, James Madison of Virginia proposed a dozen amendments to the Constitution, and Congress approved ten of them in September 1791. They took effect in December of that year.[4] These first ten amendments to the Constitution became known as the Bill of Rights. It's important in understanding the investigative process to know that the Bill of Rights restricts actions of the government (for example, the police) against individuals. It's the Bill of Rights, particularly the Fourth, Fifth and Sixth Amendments and associated legal decisions that are the engine that drive the actions the police can and can't take. Every detainment, arrest, search, seizure, interview and interrogation is limited in some way by federal, state, and local court cases stemming from one or more of the first ten amendments. Therefore, it's absolutely critical that you have a thorough understanding of them.

The Fourth Amendment

The right of the people to be secure in their persons, houses, papers and effects, against unreasonable searches and seizures, shall not be violated, and no warrants shall issue, but upon probable cause supported by oath or affirmation, and particularly describing the place to be searched, and the persons or things to be seized.

The laws related to searching a person place or thing and to arrest are covered by the Fourth Amendment. Notice the use of the words **probable cause.** In order to make a valid arrest (seizure) or to search a particular person, place, or thing, a police officer needs to have probable cause—*facts and circumstances which would lead a reasonable person to believe that a crime is being, has been, or will be committed.* Note the use of the present, past, and future tense in this definition. If a police officer observes a crime *committed in his/her presence*—Joe strikes Paul in the face with his fist, breaking Paul's nose—then the officer may, in most states, arrest Joe without an arrest warrant signed by a judge.

In most states, police can make an arrest without a warrant based on probable cause. Photo courtesy of Tri-Tech, Inc.

If Joe strikes Paul in the face with his fist, breaking Paul's nose, and a police officer was not present but was called to the scene a short time after this occurred (past), this is an example of a crime that *has been committed.* The officer did not see the crime occur. In most states, if Joe can be located a short time after the incident based on speedy information from Paul, then Joe can be arrested without an arrest warrant based on probable cause. This ability of the police in most states to arrest without an arrest warrant signed by a judge is especially true if the assault was a felony.

An example of a crime that *will be committed* is if a confidential reliable informant told a detective that a bank robbery was being planned and that the informant had recently been present in an apartment and heard three other men discussing robbing the bank. He also observed the men viewing diagrams of the bank, alarm codes and escape routes, and he saw weapons in the apartment to be used in the bank robbery.

So the definition of what constitutes a crime, felony, misdemeanor and violation; corpus delicti; and elements of a crime are crucial to understanding the circumstances under which an officer can make an arrest.

Arrest

We have already discussed the definition of what constitutes a crime. However, for a police officer to make an arrest—with or without an arrest warrant signed by a judge—the officer must be able to conclude that there is a *reasonable probability* that an offense has been committed and that the person is in fact a criminal participant (*State v. Gant*, 231 Conn. 43 [1994]). A shortened version of the definition of probable cause often used to train police officers is *less than proof, but more than mere suspicion that a crime is being, has been, or will be committed.* Thus, probable cause requires a higher standard than *reasonable suspicion* but less than the standard of *proof beyond a reasonable doubt,* which is required for conviction in court. Probable cause is a series of facts and circumstances—a step-by-step progression—which, by themselves or in combination, may be used by a reasonably prudent person to believe that a crime was committed and the suspect to be arrested committed the crime. Another definition of probable cause is *rational grounds of suspicion, supported by circumstances sufficiently strong in themselves to warrant a cautious man in believing the accused to be guilty.* (*Brinegar v. United States*, 338 U.S. 161 [1949]).

PROBABLE CAUSE FACTORS

1. Flight
2. Furtive movements
3. Hiding
4. Attempt to destroy evidence
5. Resistance to officers
6. Admissions or confessions
7. Evasive answers
8. Unreasonable explanations
9. Fingerprint or DNA identification
10. Hair follicle identification
11. Handwriting comparisons
12. Fabric comparisons
13. Identification of a suspects by a witnesses
14. Ballistics
15. Contraband or weapons in plain view
16. Criminal record
17. Hearsay information
18. Police training and experience
19. Unusual or suspicious behavior
20. Footprints, blood splatter evidence, tire impressions, etc.

A partial list of guilt-laden or other facts that may be used to build probable cause

There are many different definitions of what constitutes an *arrest.* One definition of an arrest is *the taking of a person into custody for violation of any law, ordinance, regulation, or bylaw of the state.* Another is *the action of taking a person into custody for the purpose of charging him or her with a crime.* [5] Whichever definition we use, arrest is a "seizure" of a person under the Fourth Amendment.

In addition to the probable cause requirements, an arrest has three basic elements:

1. Authority

2. Intention

3. Custody

The following story illustrates all three elements:

WAR STORY

Many years ago, I was walking a beat in Hartford, Conn. On the beat was a large park, and I was strolling along one of its paths—in full uniform, of course—swinging my nightstick to and fro in celebration of a gorgeous spring day (a police officer in his jurisdiction with the authority to arrest). A very elderly woman sitting on one of the park benches feeding the pigeons waved me over.

"Top of the morning to you, ma'am," said I to the lady, tipping me hat.

She cocked her head and motioned me closer and pointed. "You see that man over there by the fountain? He has a .45 automatic under his coat in a holster just over his back pocket," said she. I looked over at the man, who was about twenty feet away and was now slowly walking in the opposite direction. "How do you know that?" I asked.

"I saw it. I was in the army for thirty-five years and I carried a .45 every day. I know guns, and I know one when I see it." I nodded, seeing the elderly woman in a new light.

I rapidly made my way along the path, and as I closed in on the man, he looked over his shoulder. His face showed alarm, and he increased his pace almost to a trot. I yelled, "Hey, buddy, I want to talk with you." The man began to run, and I started running after him. The man ran out of the park into a line of traffic, narrowly missing being hit by several cars. I saw the man take out a gun, and as he ran by a mailbox, he opened the lid and tossed the gun in. I yelled, "You're under arrest!" and then tackled him. After a brief struggle, I managed to get him in handcuffs.

A list of the *building blocks*, or **elements of probable cause**, which gave me the authority to arrest, looks like this:

1. I was a readily identifiable police officer, on duty in my jurisdiction.

2. It was daytime—no vision obstructions.

3. I was contacted by a citizen who reported a possible crime.

4. The citizen appeared to be credible—she related information about a possible crime based on her prior experience (army, guns) and specific personal observations (man carrying gun).

5. The citizen had no discernible reason to lie or gain anything from reporting her observations.

6. As I approached the man, he looked at me with an expression of alarm, increased his pace and began moving away quickly.

7. I told the man I wanted to speak with him, at which point he ran away from me, out of the park and into a line of traffic, narrowly missing being hit by several cars.

8. I observed the man take out a gun and, as he ran by a mailbox, open the lid and toss it in.

Whether or not probable cause exists in each case is determined by the **totality of circumstance surrounding the act or acts in question** (*State v. Atkinson*, 235 Conn. 748 [1996]).

Did I have facts and circumstance that would lead a reasonable person to believe that a crime had been committed and that this person committed the crime? You bet. Did I have the authority and intention to arrest the man? I did. Did I take the man into custody with the intent of bringing him before a court to answer for a crime? Absolutely.

Did I have a warrant for the man's arrest signed by a judge? No. A crime was committed in my presence. It's important to note that the facts gathered prior to an arrest in support of probable cause cannot be used *post facto*. Had I not observed the suspect place the gun in the mailbox and arrested him *prior to its discovery,* I could not use the later discovery of the gun in support of the probable cause to arrest him.

There are many intricate layers in the law relative to authority, intention, and custody. For example, what if a police officer is pursuing a fleeing felon in a motor vehicle and the felon drives the car over the city or state line into another city or state where the officer would not normally have jurisdiction? In most states, this circumstance is covered under "hot pursuit," and the officer carries jurisdictional authority to arrest into the city or state.

What if the officer is in another jurisdiction in hot pursuit and loses sight of the suspect? Once again, the standard is what would be reasonable and prudent under the totality of circumstance. How serious is the crime? Would ten minutes of searching and then finding the felon be reasonable? How about thirty minutes, an hour, five hours? Time and time again throughout legal interpretations of the law, you will read the words "reasonable and prudent" or "were the officer's actions reasonable given the circumstances?" Later in this text we will discuss this reasonable and prudent standard again when we discuss search and seizure.

Arrest with a Warrant

Thus far we have been discussing arrest without a warrant signed by an impartial magistrate (judge). From a strict interpretation of the Constitution, an arrest can be made only with a warrant. But things have changed since 1789, and through the years the courts have made many exceptions to this requirement. Now, the majority of arrests in the United States are made without a warrant.

There are several advantages to securing a warrant for a person's arrest. From a social contract point of view (utilitarianism), it supports the fact that arrests are subject to judicial scrutiny, and obtaining a warrant ensures the separation of the executive (police) and the judicial branches of government. Another advantage is that when police officers obtain an arrest warrant, a judge has determined there is probable cause to believe a crime has been committed and that a particular person committed it. This helps to negate charges by defense council relative to the legality of the arrest, as an independent evaluation of the evidence in support of probable cause to arrest has taken place.

An arrest warrant is an order of the court instructing any officer within the court's jurisdiction to arrest an individual and bring him or her before the court to answer for a crime. Normally, arrest warrants can be served anywhere in a state. This is another example of a situation in which the officer brings jurisdiction into another town, where he/she would not usually be able to arrest a person. Although a limited number of jurisdictions allow for verbal authorization, in most cases the application for an arrest warrant must be written and supported by a sworn affidavit on which the officer(s) relates probable cause factors indicating that an identifiable person committed a specific crime or crimes.

In the United States, blanket or John Doe warrants are not allowed. The description of the suspect "must be specific enough to permit an officer not acquainted with the case to identify the person to be arrested with reasonable certainty."[6] Science has now progressed far enough to allow DNA evidence to meet this "reasonable certainty" standard, and warrants are now being issued in several states based on a DNA profile without the subject's name.

Detainment

The police can detain a person if they have ***reasonable suspicion*** the person has committed or is about to commit a crime.

What about other situations? It's Saturday night, and the local pub is full of people. An argument leads to a man's pulling a gun and shooting another man to death. Police respond to the scene. Hundreds of people are in the bar and its adjoining parking lot. Can a police officer legally detain all of these people? Can officers make people remain at the scene? Not unless the officer has a reasonable, articulable suspicion that one or more of the persons was involved in the shooting.

Although a 1983 Supreme Court decision (*Florida v. Royer*, 460 U.S. 491) found that law enforcement officers do not violate the Fourth Amendment by approaching an individual on the street or in another public place and asking that person if he/she is willing to answer some questions, it becomes a "seizure" of the person if, in view of all the circumstances surrounding the incident, a reasonable person would believe he/she is not free to leave (*U.S. v. Mendenhall*, 446 U.S. 544 [1980]).

In police training, we often describe this as "depriving a person of their freedom of movement in a significant way." This is quite different from what's become known as a "Terry stop," "stop and frisk" or "field interrogation." In a 1968 Supreme Court decision (*Terry v. Ohio*, 392 U.S. 1), the court ruled that a police officer observing unusual conduct and suspecting a crime is about to be committed may "frisk" a suspect's outer clothing for dangerous weapons. Thus a police officer (without probable case) can make a brief detention of an individual for the purpose of investigating suspicious activity. Under the Terry doctrine, a police officer who has a "reasonable and articulable suspicion" that the person stopped may be armed can "pat down" the outer clothing of the person. Then, if the officer sees of feels an item which he/she reasonably believes is a weapon, he/she can go beyond the outer clothing and seize the item. Although this is a "limited search," an officer may place his/her hands in the suspect's pockets and under the suspect's outer clothing.[7] If the officer makes a valid Terry stop and then conducts a frisk of a person, believing that person to be armed, then the fruit of that search (the gun) is admissible in court, and the person could be charged with an offense. In a 1993 ruling (*Minnesota v. Dickerson*, 113 S.Ct. 2130), the Supreme Court expanded the scope of *Terry v. Ohio* to what has become known as the "plain feel" doctrine. Under this ruling, a police officer who makes a valid Terry stop and subsequently frisks an individual may seize items detected through the officer's sense of touch as long as the touch makes it "immediately apparent" that the item is contraband.

Consider the previous scenario with the lady in the park who reported to me she observed a man a short distance away who had a ".45 automatic under his coat in a holster just over his back pocket." In our original scenario, the man took flight and was observed stashing the gun in a mailbox. However, based on the information from a credible citizen, had I approached the man and had he not run away, could I have detained him (Terry stop) and then conducted a frisk to determine whether he was armed? The man could have a permit to carry a weapon, but did I have "reasonable and articulable suspicion"that, absent a permit, a crime had been committed and this person was armed? Yes, I did.

If, after frisking the man and removing the weapon from his possession (removing the danger to myself and others), a subsequent investigation revealed he had a valid permit to carry a concealed weapon, then he could go on his way. The courts will look at the "totality of circumstances" to determine whether my actions were reasonable and prudent given the circumstances.

Of course, there are many cases that are legal and proper when the police properly detain (seize) people without their consent. Consider the following situation: It's winter and bitterly cold outside. At two in the morning, a police officer on vehicular patrol observes an elderly man walking down the sidewalk without a shirt or coat, talking to himself. Would it be proper for the officer to stop the man and inquire if he was okay? If it were obvious to the officer the man was suffering from Alzheimer's disease and didn't know where he was, would it be proper for the officer to place the man in the rear, locked section of his cruiser? What if the man didn't want to get in the cruiser? Would it be proper for the officer to use reasonable force to place the elderly man in the cruiser? Would it be proper to handcuff the elderly man to prevent him from injuring himself? Can the officer frisk the elderly man to make certain his does not have anything on his person he could use to harm himself? Of course. In this case, the officer later determined the man walked away from a nursing home a short distance away and brought him back.

Don't we have an expectation that the police will protect people? The officer was not in the arrest mode, but in the "helping, public service mode." There was no intent on the officer's part to arrest, and the officer's actions were reasonable and prudent given the totality of the circumstances. Don't forget, the Constitution protects people against unreasonable searches and seizures, not reasonable searches and seizures.

All of this information is important in a text about criminal investigation because what we do and how we do it determines whether evidence seized during detainment or arrest or as a result of questioning or interrogation is admissible at trial.

Unless you have a thorough knowledge of the legal ramifications of your actions, all of your hard work will be for naught. All of the forensic science in the world is useless if the evidence is illegally seized and inadmissible at trial..

Search and Seizure

The Fourth Amendment of the Constitution protects people against unreasonable searches and seizures of their "persons, houses, papers, and effects." It also states that "no warrants shall be issued but upon probable cause, supported by oath or affirmation, and particularly describing the place to be searched and the person or things to be seized." (*Minnesota v. Dickerson*, 113 S. Ct. 2130 [1993]).

The United States Supreme Court established a further standard under the Fourth Amendment called the ***Exclusionary Rule***, which prohibits the use in court of evidence seized in violation of the Fourth Amendment. Thus, if the police illegally obtain evidence, it can't be used against an accused in court.

Central to criminal investigation is that police officers search for and then seize evidence relating to a crime. The police routinely search persons, homes, cars, crime scenes and businesses. Investigative knowledge and application of how to legally search a person, place or thing and then properly seize evidence is a basic requisite to the investigative process.

Our previous discussion of probable cause is important here because, with some notable exceptions, all searches, whether with or without a search warrant, must be supported by probable cause. In a 1983 Supreme Court decision (*Illinois v. Gates*, 462 U.S. 213), the court found that judges reviewing search warrants and supporting affidavits by the police asking to search a particular person, place or thing, may make a common-sense decision based on the ***totality of circumstances*** as to whether the circumstances in the affidavit indicate a "fair probability" that contraband (among other things) will be found in a particular place.

Notice the use of the words "fair probability." Many scholars have opined that fair probability is slightly less that probable cause and similar to ***preponderance of evidence***, which is the standard of proof used in civil court and often explained as "more likely than not."

In many states, the affidavit in support of the search warrant application requires that two officers swear that sufficient facts—probable cause—exist when

1. A crime has been, is being, or will be committed.

2. A particularly described item of seizable evidence exists and is connected to the crime.

3. A particularly described item is at the present time located in the place to be searched (*Mapp v. Ohio*, 367 U.S. 643 [1961]).

Particularity

The search warrant must particularly describe the person or place to be searched. This means that the person or place must be distinguishable from all others. For example, a search warrant for 432 Main Street may not be sufficient. In which town, city or state is 432 Main Street located? Is it a single-family home or a large apartment complex with forty different apartments? A more particular description might be 432 Main Street, a single-family, cape-style home, located on the west side of Main Street, along with the name of the city and state, with a gold-colored placard engraved with "The Sullivans" on the front door. Court cases are replete with instances in which searches and resulting evidence have been nullified because of a failure to meet this Fourth Amendment protection.

Simply because a judge signs a search warrant doesn't mean it will not be subject to later judicial review. The same holds true for obtaining a warrant to search a person. As we previously discussed, a search warrant must be specific enough to permit an officer not acquainted with the case to identify the person to be searched with reasonable certainty. Thus, a warrant for José Melendez would not meet the particularity requirement. A warrant for José Melendez, date of birth 1/28/75, a Hispanic male, approximately 5'8" in height, with a word "homeboy" tattooed on his right hand would sufficiently identify this José Melendez from the thousands of others with the same name.

Similarly, what the police are searching for must meet the Fourth Amendment requirement to particularly describe the thing(s) to be seized. This limits the extent of the search to the item(s) listed in the search warrant application, For instance, if the police obtained a warrant to search a particular home for .38-caliber, chrome-plated revolver, serial number A49572, this description would meet the particularity requirement.

However, the search of the home must end when the item is found. So if the homeowner were to immediately provide officers with the location of the gun in the home and they were to locate it right away, the item listed on the search warrant has been seized and the police must stop searching. Nevertheless, a search for heroin, glassine bags, scales, packaging devices, records of sale, and money derived from the sale of narcotics would be very extensive and would allow officers a very broad search that one could argue would be almost limitless in scope.

Another way to look at what the police can search for with a search warrant is to think of general categories, such as fruits of a crime, instrumentalities of a crime, contraband, or mere evidence.

Fruits of a Crime	Money taken in a bank robbery
Instrumentality of a Crime	Weapons used in the bank robbery
Contraband	Illegal narcotics or controlled substances
Mere Evidence	Hair, fibers, semen, fingerprints, etc.

Exceptions to the Fourth Amendment Search Warrant Requirement

Through the years, a variety of court cases have carved out some very limited exceptions to the Fourth Amendment requirement that the police obtain a search warrant prior to searching a person, place, or thing. There are seven distinct exceptions to the Fourth Amendment search warrant requirement: exigent circumstances, search incidental to a lawful arrest, consent, plain view, caretaker function, impounded vehicles, and motor vehicle.

Exigent Circumstances

The word ***exigent*** means "emergency." A police officer on patrol in the early hours of the morning who observes a multi-tenant apartment building on fire can forcibly enter the front door of the building to warn and evacuate tenants. While doing so, if the officer observes smoke pouring out from under one of the apartment doors, knocks and receives no response, the officer certainly doesn't have to go get a search warrant to break down the door and rescue an elderly person in a wheelchair. The key here and in other cases is *time and need*. The officer does not have time to get a warrant, and there is an immediate risk of harm to the public requiring immediate official action.

There are many other situations under which officers do not need to secure a search warrant in order to act. If shots are being fired at the officers and they have to conduct a search of a premises or a building, then they and the public are in *imminent danger*, and they do not have time to secure a warrant. Likewise, when an officer has probable cause to believe that evidence of a crime is about to be destroyed, or when an officer is in hot pursuit of an escaping criminal who runs into a house, a warrant is not required. In *Mincey v. Arizona* (1978), the Supreme Court ruled that officers do not have to delay a search if to do so would endanger their lives or the lives of others.

Search Incident to Lawful Arrest

In a 1973 Supreme Court Decision (*United States v. Robinson*, 17 414 U.S. 218), the court stated, "It is the fact of the lawful arrest which establishes the authority to search, and we hold that in the case of the lawful custodial arrest a full search of the person is not only an exception to the warrant requirement of the Fourth Amendment, but is also a 'reasonable' search under the Amendment. The arrest must be valid under law. This is true even if the officer and the person being arrested are of the opposite gender. The officer must be able to specifically articulate probable cause that the person committed a crime and there must have been an intention on the part of the officer to arrest prior to the search of the person."

In other words, an officer can't search, find narcotics, and then arrest for possession of the narcotics based on that search. The search of a person who is under arrest is subject to the "areas under that person's immediate control" (*Chimel v. California*, 395 U.S. 752 [1969]).

A simple example might be a person whom the police observe to have committed a crime—a man punches another man in the mouth—and places him under arrest. Just prior to punching the man, the police see the suspect take off a coat and place it on the hood of a car next to him. There is no one else near the coat. Is the coat under the suspect's immediate control? Yes. Can the police search the pockets of the coat prior to handing it to the suspect after he has been arrested? Yes. If marijuana is found in the coat, can the police place an additional charge relative to the contraband on the man in addition to the assault? Yes—they arrested the man, and it was the search after or incidental to the arrest that discovered the marijuana.

WAR STORY

Here is a more complicated example of search incident to arrest. When I was assigned to the narcotics squad, the department received complaints about drug dealing on a particular street. One of the complainants was the owner of an apartment building overlooking the area in which drugs were being sold. He offered to let us use a vacant apartment on the third floor to set up a surveillance. My partner and I arrived at the apartment before dawn so we wouldn't be "made" and set up a long, 35mm camera lens on a tripod, hoping to take some snapshots of the drug dealers.

Around eight in the morning, we saw a man walking down the street carrying a folding lawn chair. We watched him go into a vacant lot about twenty feet from the street, look all around, and then remove a brown paper bag from under his jacket, take something out of the bag, pry up a large rock, and place the paper bag under the rock. He then walked to the sidewalk, unfolded the lawn chair and sat down.

Within a short amount of time, the man had quite a business going. Cars would pull over to the curb, the man would get up, approach the car, take a few twenty dollar bills from the car's driver or passenger and, in return, give the customer a couple of small glassine bags filled with a white powder. Every so often, the man would return to the rock, lift it up, and remove a handful of small glassine bags from the brown paper bag and put the paper bag back under the rock.

This is pretty common for street-level drug dealers. They think if the police arrest them with only a couple of bags of coke or dope, they can be charged only with possession instead of the more serious possession with intent to sell.

Eventually, we had seen enough and arrested the man. In a search subsequent to his arrest, we found two small glassine bags containing white powder in his jacket pocket, plus a wad of cash. We conducted a field test on the white powder which came back as positive for cocaine. I went over and lifted up the rock and in the brown paper bag found over two hundred glassine bags of coke.

Was the brown paper bag under the rock in the man's possession? Was the brown paper bag under the rock, which was twenty feet away from where we arrested the man, "within his immediate control"?

The man's defense attorney argued that the even if the arrest and search of his person were valid, the brown paper bag found under the rock was not under his client's immediate control.

However, the court found the scope of our search to be reasonable given the totality of the circumstances, and the brown paper bag to be within the suspect's control. The man was convicted.

Consent

Police may search without a search warrant if they have **consent** from a person who has the authority to give it. Probable cause is not required if the consent is "knowingly and intelligently given." Searching a person or place with consent always presents problematic legal issues because of the heavy burden of the police and prosecutor to prove the defendant *voluntarily* consented to a search and no threats of any kind were made. It is difficult to overcome the question of why a defendant would voluntarily consent to a search by the police of his or her home, knowing there are twenty pounds of marijuana on the bed in the bedroom.

These are some of the same legal issues officers are confronted with in conducting interviews and interrogations and in taking statements and confessions. The legal issues in consent searches are

1. *Who can consent to a search of what?*

2. *What constitutes voluntary consent?*

3. *What limitations does the law im pose on those conducting the search?*[8]

A child cannot consent to a search. The legal definition is associated with age, so you need to know at what age a person is considered to be a child in your state. In Connecticut, anyone under the age of sixteen is considered a child and incapable of giving consent. Generally speaking, it would be difficult to prove a person voluntarily gave consent if he or she were impaired in any way— intoxication by alcohol or drugs, mental condition, traumatized due to injury, or if there were a language barrier, etc. All of us in law enforcement have been in the situation of speaking to a forty-year-old person, but it's immediately apparent the person has the mental capacity (due to psychological and/or genetic dysfunction) of a ten-year-old. If the officer recognizes the defect, so will the court, and it will be difficult to show the person knowingly and voluntarily consented to a search.

In a 1990 Supreme Court decision (*Illinois v. Rodriguez*, 497 U.S. 177), the court ruled that a person can consent to a search if "the facts available to the officer at the time of entry warrant a man of reasonable caution to believe the consenting party has authority over the premises." So if my brother and his wife go to Florida for the winter and leave me the key to their home to check it from time to time, do I have authority over the premises? Yes, I do. Most police departments have developed a legal form with carefully written language (Consent to Search form), which officers carry and have people fill out and sign indicating their consent to search and that the consent was voluntary. It's also a good idea to have this form witnessed by a person who is not a police officer.

However, in a 1973 Supreme Court decision (*Schneckloth v. Bustamonte*, 412 U.S. 218), the court ruled that officers do not have to specifically advise an individual he or she does not have to consent. A person's consent, even if in writing, can be withdrawn at any time, and the police must stop searching. A parent may consent to the search of a child's room where no rent is paid, but a hotel manager or landlord may not provide legal consent to search unless the room or apartment is abandoned

Although there are plenty of cases in which consent searches may make sense from a street-level point of view, I highly recommend obtaining a search warrant whenever time and circumstances permit.

Plain View

Another exception to the search warrant requirement is the ***plain view doctrine***. In 1968, the Supreme Court ruled in *Harris v. United States* (390 U.S. 234), and later in *Horton v. California* (496 U.S. 128 [1990]), that when an officer has a right to be where he or she is, anything an officer observes in plain view is not the product of a search and is admissible as evidence. If the police have probable cause to believe something observed is contraband, stolen property, or other evidence of a crime, the police can seize it if they are lawfully in a place and see it.

WAR STORY

Years ago, I was in uniform walking a beat in a section of the city that had a mixture of business establishments and homes. As I was walking down a city sidewalk, I saw a man in his pajamas watering four large marijuana plants on his front porch. (I'm not making this up.)

Did I have a right, as a police officer, to be where I was? Yes. Did I observe contraband with my own eyes? Yes. I arrested the man and seized the marijuana plants.

An officer stops a motor vehicle for a traffic offense and requests the operator produce his license, registration, and insurance card. If the operator opens up the glove compartment and a gun drops out onto the floor, then the gun was in plain view. If the operator has a marijuana cigarette smoldering in the ashtray, then the marijuana cigarette is in plain view. Officers may also enhance their vision by using a flashlight, binoculars or other devices. It's now becoming common for cities and towns to have cameras in public places and officers in a kiosk viewing television monitors. The officer is in a place he/she has a legal right to be, viewing a public area not protected under the Fourth Amendment.

Caretaker Function

There are situations in which police officers find lost property, valuables or dangerous items. Citizens come across them also and either report their locations or turn them over to the police.

Consider a traffic accident involving three cars in which the drivers are seriously injured and brought to the hospital. Items from the cars are strewn along a highway. An officer picks up an expensive briefcase in the roadway that he has reason to believe is from one of the cars involved in the accident. The officer doesn't know from which car the briefcase came and opens it to determine whether he can identify the owner by its contents. He wants to know whether he can return it or properly label it so the owner came claim it later from police headquarters.

The briefcase has two pounds of cocaine in it, along with items identifying the owner. The owner of the briefcase is one of the persons brought to the hospital. Was the officer's search of the briefcase" reasonable given the totality of circumstances? Sure.

People report finding everything from hand grenades to alligators. So do police officers. Imagine a disaster such as Hurricane Katrina in New Orleans. Police officers in boats saw all kind of valuables floating by. If they had the time and equipment, they would have retrieved them and returned them if the owner could be identified.

WAR STORY

Speaking of alligators, Hartford, Conn. used to have a zoo called Sherwood Forest in Keney Park. I was walking a beat one night on a city street quite a distance from the zoo. It was pouring rain, and I had ducked into an alcove to have a cigarette and keep a watchful eye for the sergeant because we were not supposed to smoke in public. An old vagrant was sitting against the wall in the alcove drinking some wine from a bottle partially hidden in a small paper bag. He was half popped, and we started talking about the old boxers from Hartford—Willie Pep and guys like that—which kind of perked him up.

My back was partially turned from the street, and all of a sudden he kind of raised up on his toes and looked over my shoulder. His face had an astonished expression and I turned to see a huge alligator walking down the sidewalk swishing his tail back and forth. If that wasn't bad enough, the alligator had a dog in its mouth and a satisfied grin on his face.

When I called it in over the radio, the Irish dispatcher asked me whether I had "been tipping it a little bit," meaning, of course, the bottle.

That's the caretaker function. We find lost things.

Impounded Vehicle Inventory

Cars are towed by the police all the time. The question is whether a towed vehicle can be searched. If someone is arrested and the car is towed, do the police have an obligation to protect the person's property in the vehicle? In 1976, the court ruled in *South Dakota v. Opperman* (428 U.S. 364) that impounded vehicles may be searched and inventoried using standard police procedures to secure the vehicles and its contents.

This is similar to the caretaker function exception to the Fourth Amendment. If an officer were to find contraband or evidence of a crime during the inventory of the vehicle and had probable cause to believe it belonged to the registered owner or an arrested person, then that could be the basis for an arrest.

The court has pointed out that the inventory search cannot be used as a pretext for discovering incriminating evidence. It's best if the department has a written policy requiring officers to inventory *all* vehicles towed and impounded. Obtain a search warrant if you want to search a vehicle that is part of a crime scene. For example, if a person were found to have been shot to death in a vehicle after the body has been removed, you certainly would want to obtain a search warrant to thoroughly process the car for items of evidentiary value.

Motor Vehicle Exception

Through the years, Fourth Amendment protections against searching motor vehicles have diminished. In 1925, the Supreme Court ruled in *Carroll v. United States* (2657 U.S. 132) that if there were probable cause for an officer to secure a search warrant, it might not be practical to do so because the vehicle is movable.

In a 1981 case (*New York v. Belton*, 453 U.S. 454), the court ruled that when a police officer arrests a person in a vehicle, the officer may search the vehicle's passenger compartment, including any open or closed containers. This does not include the trunk of the vehicle.

In 1999, the Supreme Court ruled in *Maryland v. Dyson* (527 U.S. 465) that a warrantless search of a vehicle may be justified if an officer has probable cause to believe the vehicle contains contraband, controlled substances or criminal evidence. The court reiterated that although the search is limited to areas where the officer has probable cause to believe an item may be located, the search extends to any container found that might contain the item. Note the probable cause requirement: Stopping a motor vehicle for a routine violation does not rise to the level of probable cause to believe the vehicle contains contraband, controlled substances or evidence of a crime.

Chapter One Endnotes

1. Bennett, Wayne & Hess, Karen, Criminal Investigation, 2001, 6th Edition, Wadsworth Publishing, Belmont, CA, p3.

2. Osterburg, James & Ward, Richard, Criminal Investigation—A Method for Reconstructing the Past, 2nd Edition, Anderson Publishing, Cincinnati, Ohio, 1977, p. 5.

3. Inciardi, James, Introduction to Criminal Justice, 7th Edition, Harcourt College Publishers, Orlando, FL, 2002, p. 49

4. Ibid. p.126

5. Inciardi, James, Criminal Justice, 7th Edition, Harcourt College Publishers, Orlando, FL, 2002, p. 141

6. Swanson, Charles, etal, Criminal Investigation 9th edition, McGraw Hill Publishing, Boston, Ma., 2006.p 29

7. Connecticut Law Enforcement Officers Field Manual, page 468-469.)

8. Inciardi, James, Introduction to Criminal Justice, 7th Edition, Harcourt College Publishers, Orlando, FL, 2002, p. 238

Chapter Two

The Investigative Process

What Does an Investigator Do?

A detective in a small agency might be a jack-of-all-trades, while in larger agencies, detectives are often specialists. Photo Courtesy of Tri-Tech, Inc.

There are approximately 12, 665 local police departments employing around 466,000 police officers in the United States.[1] The majority of local agencies have fewer than five full-time police officers All of these officers are investigators and will spend the majority of their careers conducting investigations into crime. When crimes are observed by an officer or reported to the police, it's usually a patrol unit assigned to the area that responds to conduct a preliminary investigation. Many cases do not require the assistance of detectives because the case is solved and/or doesn't require a sustained investigation.

An armed robbery of a package store in which the culprits are apprehended a few blocks away will involve the investigative process (arrest, seizure of evidence, processing of a crime scene, taking of written statements, etc.), but may not involve detectives at all, or they may play only an assist role.

Patrol officers are certainly qualified to handle most cases. The backbone of the police service is patrol, and patrol units are called line units because it's the officer on the street who is most responsible for the delivery of police services. Just about every other police function, including detective work, is "staff." The only reason staff exists is so patrol units will not have to spend lengthy amounts of time conducting investigations. Patrol units are supposed to be patrolling to prevent crime from occurring in the first place.

Detective work is specialized. A police department's detective force rarely is first on the scene. In the majority of cases, detectives are called to the scene (such as a murder) because the department recognizes the time involved to fully investigate the case will be extensive and/or special expertise is needed. In other cases, a patrol officer responds to the scene and conducts a preliminary investigation and gather information that which needs to be followed up on.

If our armed robbery of the package store didn't result in an arrest, further investigation might be required, which could take days or months. This is a job for a detective. Many larger departments have further specialized the investigative process into units or divisions that have been functionally divided into types of investigative work.

When I was Chief of Detectives in Hartford, Conn., we had a Crimes Against Persons Division (Homicide, Robbery, Sexual Assault, Serious Physical Assault), a Crimes Against Property Division (Burglary, Arson, Auto Theft), a Vice and Narcotics Division, a Youth Services Division (serious crimes involving juveniles), an Intelligence Division (Organized Crime and Street Gangs), and an Evidentiary Services Division (Crime Scene and Evidence Processing). Each division was commanded by a lieutenant and comprised of several sergeants and many detectives. Imagine the specialization in even larger departments, such as New York, with about 40,000 police officers; Chicago, with around 13,466; and Los Angeles, with another 9,341 officers. Smaller departments might have only one detective who handles all of these specialized tasks or is supplemented by a state agency. So, a detective in a small agency might be a jack of all trades and handle an investigation from nuts to bolts. A detective in one of the larger agencies might truly be a specialist and have received a great deal of training in a relatively narrow area, such as homicide.

Investigative Responsibilities

The primary source I use in reviewing material on criminal investigation is *Criminal Investigation – A Method for Reconstructing the Past*, written by James Osterburg and Richard Ward. This is truly a book for the practitioner and provides a good working outline of basic investigative responsibilities, which include the following:

1. Determine whether a crime has been committed.
2. Decide whether the crime was committed within the investigator's jurisdiction.
3. Discover all facts pertaining to the complaint..
   A. Determine when the crime was committed.
   B. Determine how the crime was committed.
   C. Gather and preserve physical evidence.
   D. Develop and follow up on all clues.
4. Recover stolen property.
5. Identify the perpetrator or eliminate a suspect as the perpetrator.[2]

Traits of a Good Investigator

Many books about criminal investigation spend a great deal of time listing the attributes of what makes an effective investigator. These lists often include the ability to prioritize (follow a logical investigative sequence), a high level of intelligence, ability to separate fact from opinion, multi-tasking, ability to relate well with others, and so on. Most police officers—not just detectives—possess these traits.

It's been my experience that the best detectives have a great deal of **street-level patrol experience**. There just isn't any practical substitute for spending years investigating crimes. When my students ask me whether police departments will start them off as detectives because they have a college degree and they "don't want to do the usual police work," I get so flabbergasted I don't know where to start to answer the question. Although the work is getting more and more scientific (forensics) and there have been tremendous advances in technology, we can always hire civilians who have this special expertise. The problem is that these experts don't have the investigative experience to know how to use the evidence they've uncovered. There just isn't any substitute for pounding a beat.

All the really good detectives I worked with or supervised had developed extensive knowledge of a wide range of investigative techniques—report writing, interview and interrogation, constitutional law, surveillance, narcotics, recognizing and handling evidence, etc. Each had a mentor—someone who supplemented the skills they brought with them as a good street cop—and refined that skill over several years. Every one of them investigated cases with a dogged determination. This means that they were persistent, and if you committed a crime you wouldn't want them looking for you. Every one of them knew the city and its people like the backs of their hands. The best were city-born and -bred and didn't move to the suburbs when they had finally made a few bucks.

All good detectives are lifelong students of human behavior. They have sad eyes from seeing too much. They understand human greed, avarice, jealously and all the other vices, and know to follow the money. So the "why"—the motive—behind human acts, which is so difficult to prove, is no stranger to them because they have spent their lives studying it. That's what makes a good detective.

WAR STORY

As I mentioned in the introduction, after I made detective, I was paired up with the "Cisco Kid," a veteran detective who had been on the job before I was born. Cisco was born in Hartford and went to school there, and his parents and grandparents lived there. He had a little two-room apartment in the Italian section of the city and had lived in that neighborhood all his life. He never married, but was straight and had quite a few "liaisons."

The Cisco Kid made it a point to attend every funeral in the city. White, Black, Hispanic, Italian, Irish, Polish, whatever, he went to all the wakes and brought me with him. He always came to work dressed the same: Black suit, black hat, black tie, black shirt, black shined shoes, and a fresh flower in his lapel. Pencil-thin mustache, thin as a rail. We would go into the funeral parlor and, although he didn't know anyone, he would pay his respects to the family and the deceased. We would then take a seat for about 45 minutes with the other people attending the wake. People would come up to the Cisco Kid at the wake, and he would casually remark he was a detective and hand out a business card. Someone always had a request about a son or daughter in trouble, and Cisco was a good listener. He provided small "favors" and somehow made it seem like he'd done a big service, when in reality, these people could have gotten the same results by merely going to police headquarters.

If anything happened in the city—a bank robbery, sexual assault, street mugging, etc.—the Cisco Kid only had to put out the word, and people from all walks of life would seek him out to repay the services he had rendered them by providing information. The Cisco Kid was a student of human behavior and a good listener. He was a great detective.

ANOTHER WAR STORY

Many years after the Cisco Kid had moved on to that great Detective Division in the sky, I was Chief of Detectives in Hartford, Conn. By then, the department had changed from promoting detectives through a civil service testing process to a system in which the Chief of Police would appoint officers to detective as a special assignment.

In other words, patrolmen were "made" detectives, given a gold badge that said "Detective" on it, and went up a notch in pay, but they served at the pleasure of the Chief of Police. The chief could make you one day and send you back to patrol in uniform the next. There are pros and cons to doing it this way. It allows the chief to solidify power, make a dent in the department's affirmative action goals, and in some senses can be used to motivate detectives not performing at the desired level. On the other hand some officers are promoted/designated before they are ready.

Sometimes the Chief would call to inform me he was making eight detectives and that I could chose any three I wanted, and he would pick the other five. That was his prerogative, and at least I was given three. So, among others, the Chief chose Officer Bruce Jennings (name changed to protect the innocent) and made him a "Detective." Officer Jennings had total of two years and four months on the job. He had begun to demonstrate that he had the potential to be a good cop, but was certainly not ready to be a detective. All he really could do was buy dope. I called Jennings into my office on the first minute of his first day as a detective, and after congratulating him, told him he was not qualified to be a detective. Where could I assign him? I could assign him to narcotics, but I couldn't put him in Homicide, Auto Theft, Juvenile, Intelligence, or Evidentiary Services, because he didn't have the skills necessary to do those jobs. So, I did it the old-fashioned way. I put him on rotation for three months in each of the above divisions and saw to it he was partnered with a veteran detective in each division to train him. To his credit, he saluted and said "Yes, sir!" He never complained, served his apprenticeship, and turned out to be someone I relied on for many years to come.

Conducting Preliminary Investigations

Criminal activity comes to the attention of the police either by an officer actually observing it; a report from a victim, witness, or complainant; or by an anonymous tip by telephone or mail. In the vast majority of cases, a uniformed patrol officer is sent to the scene of a reported crime by the dispatcher or comes across a crime while on patrol. The term ***preliminary investigation*** refers to the actions taken by the first officer(s) to arrive at the scene of a crime. It's not the purpose of this book to list and comment on the myriad responsibilities of the first officer(s) responding to the scene of a crime; however, there are three specific responsibilities that are critical:

1. *To provide medical care to the injured.*

The first and primary responsibility of any officer is to care for the injured, even if it means that a suspect would escape. An example: A package store is robbed, and you're right around the corner. You enter the store and see the owner has been shot in the chest but is still alive. There are civilians present, but no other police officers. You observe the robber running out the back door. Your responsibility is to the injured party. You cannot delegate this to a citizen nor can you leave and run after the robber. Radio a description of the suspect and a direction of travel to other officers, but stay and provide whatever medical attention you can until qualified medical personnel arrive. Obtain as much information as possible from the victim and any witnesses and radio that information as well.

2. *If providing medical attention is not necessary, arrest the perpetrator of the crime, and identify and detain witnesses.*

3. *Protect the crime scene.*

Every department has standing policies and procedures relative to the responsibilities of the first officers arriving at the scene of a crime. Protecting the crime scene is a critical element and the responsibility of the first responding officer after medical care has been provided and a suspect(s) arrested.

Protecting a crime scene means **making certain the crime scene is exactly as the criminal left it**. The operant idea is from "Locard's Principle of Exchange." Dr. Edmund Locard (1877-1966) was a French criminologist who posited the theory that whenever people interact with any inanimate or animate object, something is either taken away or left behind. This is what forensic science is all about. We search for evidence of the crime: hairs, fibers, semen, blood, weapons, fingerprints—the list is almost endless. The hope is that the criminal left a clue at the crime scene (or took something from the scene with him or her) that, if properly interpreted, will lead the investigator to determine what happened and who did it.

Because this book deals primarily with murders, rapes, robbery, burglary, and aggravated assault, let's blend the preliminary investigation into the responsibility to properly search the crime scene and the investigator's responsibility to conduct a follow-up investigation. Actually the term "follow-up investigation" is a misnomer because, in the case of very serious crimes, investigative personnel will respond to the scene and may engage in many of the activities normally associated with preliminary investigations. The primary difference is that the detective usually takes the case from arrival to eventual prosecution.

Securing the Crime Scene

Everyone wants to see the dead body. The press wants to see it, department brass want to have a look, and so do people living in the neighborhood. After the primary duties of medical assistance, detaining suspects and witnesses and/or arrest of the perpetrator, all unauthorized personnel should be excluded from the scene. *This is the duty of the first arriving officers and a primary responsibility of any sergeants or higher-ranking officers arriving at the scene.* Police CRIME SCENE tape, ropes, barricades, and officers should be placed at key locations to ensure the scene is protected. The crime scene is *all areas in which people connected with a crime—perpetrator, victims, witnesses—moved.* This includes the area the participant(s) moved through in order to commit the crime, while committing the crime, and in exiting the scene. In our case of the package store robber who shot the owner, the crime scene is not just the store, but the back alley the robber ran down and the fence he climbed and jumped over to reach the street.

Reasonable boundaries of the crime scene must be established and cordoned off. An officer should be delegated the task of keeping a crime scene log and entering the date and time anyone enters or leaves. Because all departments have a policy that anyone entering a crime scene is required to complete a report, this fact should be stenciled in large print across the top of the crime scene log. This tends to discourage even the most ardent sightseers. The reason for limiting access is to prevent further crime scene **contamination** or **transfer**—adding or taking away something at the crime scene that wasn't there at the time of the crime. We may only have one shot at processing a crime scene, so it's essential it be done correctly.

The lead investigator (and an evidence technician, if the department has one) should walk through the entire crime scene to determine how to proceed with evidence collection and recording the scene of the crime.

Recording the Crime Scene

It's critical for the investigation and any subsequent criminal trial that the scene of the crime be properly documented and the location of each piece of evidence recorded. This is done through investigative notes, photography and drawings. Even in small departments that do not have the resources of forensic specialists, it's relatively simple to use a digital and/or video camera to record the crime scene.

One of the advantages of video recording is the opportunity to orally narrate the recording as it's being made. It's important that the scene be photographed as it was left by the perpetrator before anything is touched or moved so that the photographs or video recording will be admissible at trial. The crime scene should be photographed from every possible angle, including points of entry and exit.

If the crime occurred inside, all rooms in the location should be photographed. In cases where a body is found, close-up photographs should be taken to indicate the position of the body relative to the crime scene. Any injury to the body or weapons should also be photographed.

When the size of an item is significant, a ruler or another object providing instant recognition of size (such as a penny or quarter) should be placed near the object and included in the photograph.

With the photographic and computer technology available today, the quality of photographs can be greatly enhanced and details of the crime scene can easily be reduced or enlarged. An advantage of digital cameras is that images can be immediately viewed and electronically distributed.

A detailed report relative to crime scene photography must be completed. Such as report would include the following:

1. *The date, time and specific location where photographs and/or video recordings were taken.*

2. *Who took the photographs and/or video recordings; the person's position and qualifications.*

3. *The specific type of camera used to take the photographs and/or video recordings.*

4. *Who was present when the photographs and/or video recordings were made.*

5. *The specific number of photographs and/or video recordings taken.*

6. *What each photograph and/or video recording is (a photograph of a .38 caliber revolver, serial number A396453 found on the floor next to the body of Delores Smith, master bedroom, 123 Washington Street, Cincinnati, Ohio.*

Crime Scene Sketches and Notes

Once the photos are taken, a rough sketch is made in order to further depict the location of evidence and anything else important at the scene of the crime. Sketching the scene of a murder is really no more difficult than drawing a diagram of a traffic accident. The same ***triangulation method*** (measuring objects from two fixed reference points and then in a straight line from each reference point to the evidence) showing the distance between objects and the dimension of an area is used, and accuracy is paramount. Use a tape measure, and designate each item of evidence with a number or letter and provide a legend in the diagram for easy reference.

The Finished Crime Scene Sketch

A finished sketch of the crime scene drawn to scale may be made later. Computerized programs are available, providing a host of drafting options that enable a professional product to be produced for court presentations. Care must be taken to retain the rough sketch along with the finished product. A good rule is to assume that anything an investigator writes or draws will be fair game in court, and it puts the case at a disadvantage when you testify that you discarded anything associated with the case.

Every police officer having anything to do with a crime scene should be required to write a detailed police report specifying exactly what he/she did. No one goes home until theirs report are completed. It may be years before the crime is solved and/or adjudicated. Memory fades, but attention to detail is critical in court. Reports, notes, drawings, photographs, and video may be the only things available to refresh an officer's memory.

Reports aren't written at the scene; officers take notes. Police officers begin learning how to take notes on the first day of the police academy. At a crime scene, the process of note taking is continuous. It's especially important that notes contain specific details describing the scene and the collection of any evidence. Who recovered the evidence, what the evidence is (gun, type and serial number, etc.) when (date and time) where (was the gun) and how (by opening a drawer, by seeing it on the floor, etc).

Searching the Crime Scene for Evidence

In the vast majority of cases, forensic specialists are not called to the scene of a crime to search for evidence. Unlike the popular television series *CSI*, regular police officers and detectives identify and collect physical evidence and package it properly for transport to a laboratory for analysis. Because physical evidence can be both visible and invisible (fingerprints), large and microscopic, the type of crime scene and the experience and training of those collecting evidence will determine what's being looked for. Although it would be impractical to list everything that could be evidence, the following are basic items common to many different types of crime scenes.

Fingerprints

Fingerprints are extraordinarily valuable as evidence because they identify a specific person. Finding your fingerprint on a gun doesn't mean you fired the weapon or shot somebody, but it's absolutely certain you touched the gun. A person's individual fingerprint ridge (***minutiae***) characteristics do not change as they age, even though the hands and fingers grow larger from infancy to adulthood. Fingerprints are not affected by gender or race. A person might attempt to alter their

Cyanoacrylate prints lifted from a battery with a black gelatin lifter. *Photo Courtesy of Tri-Tech, Inc.*

fingerprints, but the resulting scar tissue and remaining ridge characteristics will still individualize and identify the person.

Friction ridge lines are present on a person's fingers, palms and toes. Under a microscope, the ridge lines appear as pores in the skin through which sweat and body oils pass and are deposited on objects touched. When the fingerprint is invisible to the naked eye, it is known as a ***latent fingerprint***. When a fingerprint is visible to the naked eye, (after you change the oil on your car and close the hood, leaving an oily fingerprint) it's known as a ***patent fingerprint***. The individual patterns of the ridge lines, among other factors, are called ***points*** and are the basis for fingerprint identification that individualize one person from another. Although undisturbed fingerprints on some surfaces can last for many years, they are fragile and easily destroyed.

Fingerprints are classified into three categories based on general patterns. The loop is the most common. Almost two-thirds, or about 65%, of people have loop patterns on at least one finger. Another third, or about 30%, of people have a whorl pattern on a finger or a thumb. Arches are the least common, appearing on only about 5% of individuals.[3]

Fingerprints are most easily found on smooth surfaces such as glass, tabletops and the trunk lid of a car, but all surfaces at a crime scene that could retain a fingerprint must be processed. Computers have allowed us to move from the manual storage of fingerprints to converting fingerprint images into digital data. The Automated Fingerprint Identification System (AFIS) allows law enforcement to store fingerprints in a database. Computers can compare thousands of fingerprints per second. Once it is finished with the comparisons, it generates a list of prints that are closest to the search prints. A trained fingerprint expert makes the final determination whether the prints are a match.[4]

Other than the use of powders to dust the scene for fingerprints, there are other methods that allow for the obtaining of fingerprints. We can now get prints from surfaces that wouldn't yield any even a few years ago. *Iodine fuming* (heating iodine crystals until they vaporize in a closed cabinet), the use of *ninhydrin spray*, *cyanoacrylate* (superglue) *fuming*, and *fluorescents* are allowing us to locate and identify fingerprints on porous, non-porous and rough surfaces.

Cyanoacrylate (super glue) can be used to develop latent fingerprints from a variety of surfaces.
Photo Courtesy of Tri-Tech, Inc.

Blood

Blood is frequently found at crime scenes and can help to establish that a violent crime occurred. The average adult's body contains about 6 quarts, or about 5 liters, of blood. Although **age, race or sex cannot be determined** from blood samples, DNA blood analysis can now provide individual identification.

Locating and handling blood evidence is critical at a crime scene. A large pool of fresh blood next to a shooting victim is visible and easy to identify. However, small droplets of dried blood (which may resembled a rust stain) on the victims clothes at an outdoor crime scene in a wooded area may not be. The estimated time it takes blood to dry depends on the type of surface the blood is found on, the temperature (heat causes blood to dry faster); and humidity (greater humidity decreases the time it takes blood to dry). Blood tends to dry from the outside toward the middle. Because of all of these variables, estimating the time blood takes to dry isn't very accurate and may be of limited value.

Testing for blood in a laboratory is called **serology**. In the field, a test using *Hemident* (a non-destructive test for bloodstains) does not interfere with later lab testing. This type of test is similar to *narcotics reagent field testing*, which most police officers are familiar with. Any blood found at the scene must be photographed and indicated on the crime scene sketch.

Blood found at a crime scene in its liquid form should be collected with an eyedropper and placed into a test tube marked with the subjects name, case number, date, and location where it was found. Dried blood should be scraped into an evidence folder or bag identified in the same manner, and bloody clothing or other articles should be properly marked and air-dried.

Bluestar® luminescent latent bloodstain reagent identifies bloodstains without adversely affecting DNA.
Photo Courtesy of Tri-Tech, Inc.

Bloodstain pattern analysis can help determine what happened by reconstructing where a bloodstain originated and where it came to rest. Analysis can also determine with a fair degree of accuracy the type and direction of impact that created the bloodstain, number of wounds, type of weapon, positions of the victim and assailant, and direction of travel. Establishing the sequence of events through bloodstains can assist an investigator in determining a suspect's truthfulness. Computer technology can also provide quick, accurate measurements of point of origin and place of rest of bloodstains.

A 1993 monograph by Herbert L. MacDonnell titled "Bloodstain Pattern Interpretation" (Corning, N.Y.: Laboratory of Forensic Science) provides a useful list of what may be determined from the stain patterns of splattered blood:

1. *The distance between the surface bearing the stain and the origin of the blood at the time it was shed.*

2. *The point of origin of the blood.*

3. *The type of impacting object (bludgeon or gunshot) that produced the bloodstains and the direction of its force.*

4. *The movement and direction of the person(s) and/or object(s) during the shedding of blood.*

5. *The number of blows or shots; with arterial gushing, the number of heartbeats.*

6. *The position(s) of the victim and/or object(s) during the shedding of blood.*

7. *The movement of the victim and/or object(s) following the shedding of blood.*

Semen

Semen is powerful evidence in that it can link a suspect to the scene of a crime and/or to the victim and through DNA typing identify the person from which the sperm originated. *Note that it is not semen (the mixture of sperm plus other glandular secretions) that produces a person's DNA, but the spermatozoa (mature sperm cells) themselves.*

Depending on the type of crime, the locating and collection of seminal stains can be an invaluable investigative tool. Even though some seminal stains are readily visible because of their starch-like consistency, semen fluoresces under ultraviolet light, making it easier to detect.

Laboratory testing is necessary to prove its identity, and in some cases, the blood type of the individual from whom it originated can also be determined. When sperm can't be found in the stain, an ***acid phosphate test*** (phosphates are found in the liquid portion of semen) test can be conducted in the lab to determine whether semen is present.

Semen can also be used to determine whether the person is a ***secretor***, with both blood type A and B antigens in the fluid (secretors make up 80% of the population) or a ***nonsecretor***, without blood type antigens in non-blood fluid. Suspects can be ruled in or out by determining whether they are secretors or nonsecretors and whether the body fluid sample in question came from a secretor or nonsecretor.

Firearms, Bullets, and Shell Casings

A host of physical evidence can be deduced from firearms, bullets, shot pellets and slugs, shell casings, and gunshot residue. In addition, there may be fingerprints on the firearm, clips, magazine, or bullets, and/or blood and human tissue.

Several key terms are important here. The diameter of the interior of the firearms barrel between its opposing high sides is called the ***bore.*** Shotguns are smooth-bore weapons, while rifles and pistols have rifling. The **caliber** is the diameter of a bullet. When a bullet or cartridge is fired, the bullet portion separates and goes through the barrel of the firearm. Because the bullet's caliber is slightly larger than the bore, the rifling grips the bullet, causing it to rotate, usually in a right-handed direction.

The high side of the interior of the firearms barrel is called **lands** and the low sides of the firearm barrel interior is called **grooves.** The rotation of the bullet through the interior barrel of the firearm causes striations on the bullet.

When a spent bullet is located at a crime scene or from a victim the bullet can be compared with those test-fired in the laboratory through the gun. A comparison microscope is used to determine whether the recovered bullet matches those fired through the firearm in the laboratory. In cases in which a bullet is recovered, but a firearm is not, the class characteristics of a fired bullet yield information about the weapon the bullet was fired from, such as a range of makes and models that suggest the type of weapon. More often than not, fragments of bullets are recovered from a crime scene because bullets are damaged by impact with objects such as walls, floors, and human bones.

Pellets fired from a shotgun do not lend themselves to positive identification as to whether or not they were fired from a particular shotgun. The diameter of the shotgun barrel is called the **gauge**. The size and shape of a recovered **wad** (a paper or plastic wad that pushes the pellets through the barrel of the shotgun when fired) can often determine the gauge of the shotgun and/or manufacturer.

The serial number of a firearm may prove ownership and/or provide an investigator with the ability to trace a gun from its manufacturer to sale and ownership. Because of the evidentiary value of locating a firearm used in a crime, we go to great lengths in searching for the weapon. Storm drains, mailboxes, abandoned vehicles, lakes, rivers, etc. are searched, sometimes in a several-mile radius from a murder scene in an effort to find the firearm used to kill a person.

Cartridges and Shell Casings

A cartridge case holds the powder that, when ignited, forces the bullet down the chamber of the weapon and out toward the target. When the trigger on a gun is pulled, it releases the firing pin, causing it to strike the base of the cartridge case. This causes the powder in the bullet to ignite and propel the bullet forward along the barrel of the gun. In striking the cartridge case, the firing pin leaves an impression in the soft metal that can be examined under a comparison microscope.

On a center-fire type cartridge, the firing pin must strike the center of the cartridge to ignite the powder. On a rim-fire cartridge, the firing pin can strike anywhere around the base of the cartridge to ignite the powder. Marks can be made when the casing is pulled out of the chamber or when a cartridge is forced out of the weapon. Also, someone had to load the weapon, so it's always possible fingerprints can be found on a cartridge case.

The advent of computer technology has allowed for the storage of bullet and cartridge case characteristics similar to the AFIS system that is used to store fingerprints. The Integrated Ballistics Information System (IBIS), developed for use by the Bureau of Alcohol, Tobacco, Firearms and Explosives, has microscopic images of identifying characteristics found on expended bullets and cartridge casings.

In 1999, the FBI and ATF joined together to create the National Integrated Ballistics Information Network. NIBIN provides guidelines and assistance to federal, state, and local laboratories to house an automatic search system to produce databases of files from bullets and cartridge casings found at crime scenes or test-fired from weapons recovered from crime scenes. This investigative resource can be very valuable.

Gunpowder Residue

Every police officer is required to qualify at the firing range with his or her on-duty weapon. Because range qualification involves repeatedly firing the weapon, gunpowder residue will be visible on the hand used to shoot the weapon.

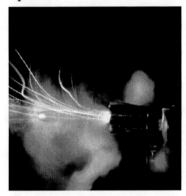

During the discharge of a firearm, escaping gases from the weapon deposit gunshot residue (GSR) on objects in the immediate vicinity.
Photo Courtesy of Tri-Tech, Inc.

When a gun is fired, the ammunition is propelled forward by the explosion of gases created by the ignition of the powder in the cartridge. However, all of the powder is never expended, and partially burned particles of gunpowder and smoke are propelled out of the barrel. Although you may not be able to see it, powder is also blown out laterally on revolvers and during the ejection of the cartridge case when an automatic pistol is fired. Objects in close range of the barrel, such as your hands when firing a gun, may receive the residue of gunpowder. This most commonly takes the form of nitrates, barium and antimony from the primer in the cartridge, which is a byproduct of the incomplete burning of powder.

Powder traces on a person's hands or clothing is powerful, but not conclusive evidence he/she fired a gun. A *Neutron Activation Analysis (NAA) test*, which uses a cotton swab saturated with dilute nitric acid, of a person's hands will detect the metal residue (barium and antimony) present when a gun is fired. Residue levels can be reduced if the person wipes off his or her hands or washes them with soap and water, but minute traces can still be detected with an

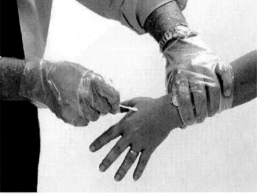

A neutron activation analysis test may detect gunpowder residue that is deposited on objects near a gun barrel, such as the shooter's hands.
Photo Courtesy of Tri-Tech, Inc.

NAA test. However, the test must be performed within a few hours of firing the weapon.[5]

Having a laboratory perform an NAA test in cases of suspected suicide with a firearm is an important investigative tool. It's critical to place clean paper bags over the hands of the deceased until the NAA test can be performed. (Plastic bags can cause condensation, which can destroy evidence.) The NAA test is also useful when suspects claim they didn't fire a gun or when a shot is fired and a gun is located amidst several suspects who all deny firing the weapon.

Estimating Distance Based on Gunshot Wounds

Previously, we discussed that objects in close range of the barrel of a firearm receive the residue of gunpowder when the gun is fired. **Contact shots** are made when the muzzle of the firearm is pressed against the body, causing gunpowder, metallic particles, and often bits of the person's clothing to be driven inward.

Contact wounds may result in the shape of the muzzle of the weapon causing an impression in the skin. The entrance wound caused by contact with a firearm is distinctive. The gases from the explosion of the weapon are forced into the wound and then back out, causing a bursting effect that often looks star-shaped, with tissue directed outward. Objects at a distance from the muzzle of a firearm receive little or no gunpowder residue.

When a person is shot at close range (but not in physical contact with the firearm) there is *tattooing* on the skin in the area where the bullet entered the body. It is this distribution of gunpowder particles around the entry wound that provides an assessment by the investigator of the distance the muzzle of the firearm was from the victim.

The powder residue pattern on the skin will vary depending on the type of weapon and ammunition used, so the accuracy of determining the distance of the weapon from the victim depending on whether a firearm is recovered and the type of ammunition is known.

In most cases, if the muzzle of the firearm was an inch or less from the victim when it was discharged, a large concentration of gunpowder particles will be observed around the bullet's entrance wound. From twelve to eighteen inches, the muzzle of the discharged firearm will produce a wider pattern of gunpowder residue.

In most cases, firearm wounds inflicted from thirty-six inches or further will not deposit noticeable gunpowder residue. The absence or presence of gunpowder residue may be important in determining whether or not the case is a suicide or a murder.

WAR STORY

At around 7:00 p.m., my partner and I were called to the residence of a single-family home in Hartford on a report by initially arriving officers of an apparent suicide.

Upon arrival, officers led us to a bedroom, where a 35-year-old male was observed lying face down on the floor with a single gunshot wound to his right temple. A .38-caliber revolver was on the floor next to the body, within inches of his right hand. The deceased was dressed in a business suit.

His wife was sobbing in the living room and had informed the first officer to arrive that she came home from work and found that her husband had shot himself. Further, her husband had been despondent for some time at being passed over for a promotion at a local insurance company.

The wife informed me that she was a nurse and other than taking her husband's pulse, she hadn't moved or touched anything in the room.

Examination of bullet wound to the right temple revealed no tattooing on the skin in the area where the bullet entered the body. The bullet was recovered in the wall, and its trajectory was not consistent with the positioning of the body, nor plausible for a suicide.

The weapon was examined: one shot fired. An empty cartridge case was in the cylinder of the revolver, along with five live bullets. Post-mortem lividity stains on the victim's body indicated he had been turned over after death. The victim's hands were bagged, and a Neutron Activation Analysis test performed.

The wife was given her Miranda warnings and presented with the evidence in the case. When she was asked whether she would submit to an NAA test on her hands, she confessed to shooting her husband following an argument about an affair he was having.

Sometimes murders are solved easily; most of the time they are not.

Marking Firearm Evidence

There are two rules for marking firearm evidence. First, make the weapon safe. Second, never place a mark directly on any type of firearm evidence.

Wear gloves. Pick up the firearm by the knurled grips or by the edge of the trigger guard. Place the firearm in a properly marked evidence container, or affix an evidence tag to the trigger guard. Bullets, cartridge cases, etc., each go into a separate evidence envelope or bag.

In the case of long guns (rifles, shotguns, etc.), affix an evidence tag to the trigger guard. **Never insert anything into the barrel of the weapon in order to pick it up.**

In cases in which a firearm is found immersed in water, do not clean or dry it. Place it in a container with the same water completely covering the weapon and transport it to the lab.

In all cases, maintain and document the chain of custody. Indicate the weapon's location on your crime scene sketch, and photograph all firearms prior to collecting them as evidence.

Bullet Trajectory and Bullets Fired Through Glass

Determining the trajectory of a bullet helps to reconstruct the crime scene and is helpful in establishing the truthfulness of suspects and witnesses.

When a bullet goes through a glass window, both *radial fracture lines* and *concentric fracture lines* develop in the glass. Radial fractures move away from the impact, and concentric lines often form a rough circle.

On the side of the window opposite the side the bullet entered is usually a cone-shaped area. If the cone-shaped area is on the inside, the bullet was most likely fired from the outside. Likewise, if the cone-shaped area is on the outside, the bullet was most likely fired from the inside. Photographs should be taken of the window detailing the fractures to the glass.

Determining the path of a bullet hole (line of fire or trajectory) though glass or other objects may be possible by sighting through the hole to trace the path back to the location where the bullet was fired from if the path of the bullet wasn't altered by striking another object. At night, you can shine a flashlight through the bullet hole to trace the path of the bullet, or you can use a laser projector for the same purpose.

Stab and Incise Wounds

Stab wounds occur when a knife of similar object is thrust into the body and pulled out.   Photo Courtesy of Tri-Tech, Inc.

A sharp-edged instrument, such as a razor, razor blade or knife, produces a *cutting or incise wound.* The wound is typically narrow at the edges and wide in the middle. These types of wounds are often found on the face, legs and arms. Forceful cutting wounds to the area around the throat are more likely to cause death than those meant to injure or disfigure.

A *stab wound* is when a knife or similar object is thrust into the body and pulled out (sometimes repeatedly), causing damage to vital organs and /or internal bleeding. The shape and size of the stab wound depend on the shape, size and sharpness of the blade. When victims attempt to defend themselves from attack by an assailant's knife or other weapon, *defense wounds* may be visible on the palms of the hands, fingers and forearms.

Strangulation

Strangulation is the constriction of the area around the throat until the natural flow of blood and air to the brain ceases. During strangulation, a person loses consciousness in approximately 10 to 15 seconds.[6]

Ligature Strangulation

A ligature is something used to tie or bind something A wide range of devices, such as ropes, neckties, cords, and undergarments, are used to put pressure around the neck and, using force, tighten the constriction, causing death by lack of blood and oxygen supply to the brain. Although many variables affect the marks left by a ligature on the neck (the type of ligature, amount of force used by the assailant and/or resistance by the victim), a ligature wound causes a furrow or grove that may be either quite prominent or very faint, depending on the type of ligature and amount of force used.

Manual Strangulation

Pressure from the hands or forearm against the neck causes the airway to be blocked, and oxygen and blood can't reach the brain. There may be contusions, scratches, abrasions and fingernail marks on the victim's skin. People can't strangle themselves because, upon losing consciousness, the pressure on the neck would be released and the person would regain consciousness. Almost all ligature and manual strangulations are murders.

Tool Marks

When a burglar inserts a screwdriver or crowbar into the frame of a window or door, some sort of indent mark is left on the soft wood. This is called a **tool mark**. Any time a tool comes into contact with an object, it leaves some type of mark: an impression, scrape or gouge.

The marks left should be photographed. The mark itself probably can't be individualized without the recovery of a tool, but careful examination may yield class characteristics to indicate a high probability that a screwdriver, for example, was used.

If the tool is recovered (you catch a burglar running from the scene with a pry bar still in his hand), the pry bar can be examined under a comparison microscope with the impression left at the scene, and the examiner could testify that, in his opinion, the pry bar the burglar was carrying made the impression in the window frame of the home that was burglarized. It would be ideal to remove the window frame to bring to the lab for comparison, but this may not be practical unless the crime was especially heinous.

Shoe and Tire Impressions

In many cases, the area around an impression and the impression itself can be readily removed for casting.

Photo Courtesy of Tri-Tech, Inc.

I once had a burglar jimmy a window into a business and step through the window onto the top of a desk, leaving a perfect sneaker impression. I was able to lift a perfect impression of the sneaker off the desk after enhancing it with fingerprint dusting powder.

Most police officers have investigated traffic accidents where the driver evaded after striking another car or pedestrian. When the car is located, inspection of the area of impact sometimes reveals pieces of fabric or tissue from the pedestrian or paint from the other vehicle.

All of us have had cases involving tire marks left on pavement or earth. These are examples of the types of impressions that may be found at the scene of a crime. Whatever the impression, it should first be photographed from a variety of angles before any attempt is made to collect the impression for transport to the laboratory. In many cases, the area surrounding the impression and the impression itself can be readily removed (impressions left on paper, bloody footprints on a rug or tile, etc.). Footprints and tire marks impressed in earth are best preserved through casting using **dental stone** or special forensic casting material.

Dental stone and casting materials can also be used for impressions left in the snow. Although style and make of tire, and type of shoe or sneaker print may be determined by using these methods, it's extremely difficult to individualize these types of impressions to a single source. Footprints are valuable in that they often can indicate whether a person was running or walking, carrying a heavy load, or was unfamiliar with the terrain.

Hairs and Fibers

Hairs

Locating hairs at a crime scene requires inch-by-inch searching using a strong light source. Unless the root is present for DNA analysis, hair cannot individualize a particular person. However, it's still important evidence that may link a person to the crime scene. In some cases, the body area from which hair came from can be established in the laboratory, but age and gender can't be determined from examining hair. Whether hair was dyed or bleached or forcibly removed can be determined.

With the advent of nuclear and mitochondrial DNA analysis, the search for and recovery of hair evidence at crime scenes is much more significant than it has been in the past. The uses of hair evidence in sexual assault investigations is covered in the section on conducting investigations into the crime of rape.

Fibers

There are four general classifications of fibers: animal, vegetable, mineral and synthetic. Examination of fibers can distinguish them relative to the above class characteristics. Fibers are of most use when there is physical contact between the victim and perpetrator, causing a transfer of fibers from one to the other or both. Although it's rare that fibers can be individualized as coming from a particular individual, the emphasis is on tracing the origin of the fiber.

If enough of a sample can be submitted to a lab, a determination may be made that it came from a single source. An example would be a rape victim's undergarments being partially torn off. If part of the undergarment was later found in a search warrant of a suspect's home it might be possible to match the evidence recovered at the scene (victim's torn undergarment taken as evidence at the hospital) to the partial undergarment kept as a "trophy" by the suspect if microscopic examination reveals a perfect fit at the torn edges.

DNA (Deoxyribonucleic Acid)

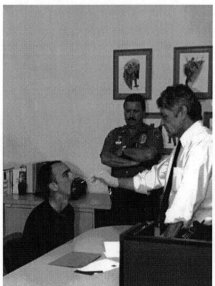

DNA can be obtained by taking a buccal swab (saliva), or from almost any other biological sample.

Photo Courtesy of Tri-Tech, Inc.

The discovery of DNA has revolutionized criminal investigation. There hasn't been a scientific discovery more important than DNA since fingerprinting. It's absolutely essential that anyone in an investigative capacity have a basic understanding of what DNA is and how it can be used. **DNA** is the abbreviation for **Deoxyribonucleic Acid**, an organic substance in the nucleus of all living cells that provides the genetic code determining a person's individual characteristics.[7] An individual's identity can be obtained from sweat, skin, blood, tissue, bone, urine, hair, semen, mucus, saliva, or almost any biological sample.

The evidence collected at the crime scene and during the medical examination of the victim is crucial to obtaining DNA evidence, which may identify the victim of a crime and/or the perpetrator. It has utility in unidentified body (skeletal remains) and missing person cases and maintains its integrity for long periods of time. It's also a powerful tool in protecting the innocent. Similar to other evidence submitted to a laboratory for analysis, the accuracy of DNA results depends on the quantity and quality of the sample(s) provided for analysis.

An example of the use of DNA was featured in a June 8, 2006, article in the Hartford *Courant* newspaper titled "Arrest in Killing Spree." For seven years during the 1980s and early 1990s, women were being raped, strangled and murdered in Bridgeport, Conn. According to the article, during that time, Emmanuel Lovell Webb "lived a seemingly routine life, sharing an apartment with his sister not far from where some of the bodies were found. Webb worked as a security guard in nearby Fairfield, Conn. Because Webb had never run afoul of the law, he never appeared on the radar screen of a task force desperately searching for clues as the body count reached 16."

In 1994, Webb moved to Georgia, where his mother lived, and according to the article, was arrested and convicted of involuntary manslaughter for sexually assaulting and strangling a woman in that state. While in a Georgia prison, Webb's DNA was entered into the FBI's national databank of convicted felons. "A random check of DNA that had been found under the fingernails of one of the victims, "Elizabeth Maxine Gandy, 33, directly matched Webb's DNA in the national database. Preliminary results indicated Webb's DNA was a match in three more of the killings." Webb is currently awaiting extradition to Connecticut from Georgia.

The Combined DNA Index System (CODIS)

DNA typing of biological material recovered from the crime scene and/or victim can be submitted to the FBI's database of DNA profiles from convicted offenders, unsolved crime scenes and missing persons. All states now have mandated the collection of DNA samples of convicted felons (depending on the state's definition of a felon), and this tool allows crime laboratories to electronically compare DNA profiles from those developed in the investigation to the ones in a national database. This is yet another example of how science and technology are merging to dramatically change criminal investigation from an art into a science. The FBI's **National Crime Information Center (NCIC)** has a comprehensive database of missing and unidentified persons linked to the **Combined DNA Index System (CODIS)**.

The following chart lists some of the evidence we have been discussing and their probative uses in conducting criminal investigations.

Evidence	Use
Fingerprints	Can individually identify a person.
Blood	Can be distinguished as to human or animal. DNA analysis can provide individual identification.
Blood Spatter Pattern Analysis	Can help determine what happened by reconstructing where a bloodstain originated and came to rest. Can also determine with a fair degree of accuracy the type and direction of impact that created the bloodstain, numbers of wounds, type of weapon, positions of the victim and assailant, and direction of travel.
Semen	Can link a suspect to the scene of a crime and/or to the victim and through DNA typing identify the person from which it originated.
Firearms	When a spent bullet is located at a crime scene or recovered from a victim, the bullet can be compared with those test-fired in the laboratory. A comparison microscope is used to determine if the recovered bullet matches those fired through the firearm. Pellets fired from a shotgun do not lend themselves to positive identification as to whether or not they were fired from a particular shotgun. The serial number on a firearm may prove ownership and/or provide an investigator with the ability
Firearms, cont'd.	to trace a gun from its manufacturer to sale and ownership.

Evidence	Use
Gunpowder Residue	A Neutron Activation Analysis test of a person's hands can detect the metal residue (barium and antimony) present when a gun is fired.
Estimating Distance Based on Gunshot Wounds	In most cases, if the muzzle of the firearm was an inch or less from the victim when it was discharged, a large concentration of gunpowder particles will be observed around the bullet's entrance wound. From twelve to eighteen inches, the muzzle of the discharged firearm will produce a wider pattern of gunpowder residue. In most cases, firearm wounds inflicted from thirty-six inches or more away will not deposit noticeable gunpowder residue.
Shoe and Tire Impressions	Style and make of tire, and type of shoe or sneaker print may be determined, but it is extremely difficult to individualize these types of impressions to a single source. Impressions can indicate whether a person was running or walking, carrying a heavy load, or was unfamiliar with the terrain.
Tool Marks	Cannot be individualized without recovery of a tool. Examination may yield class characteristics to indicate a high probability of the type of tool used.

Evidence	Use
Hairs (both pubic hair and head hair)	Cannot individually identify a person unless the root is present. Does provide strong collaborative evidence individual was at the crime scene. Can be distinguished between human and animal. May be able to determine race. May be able to establish the part of the body from which hair came.
Fibers	Limited value due to mass production of materials. In rare cases, individual identification with a high degree of certainty can be deduced.
DNA	An individual's identity can be obtained from sweat, skin, blood, tissue, bone, urine, hair, semen, mucus, saliva or almost any biological sample.

Evidence From a Legal Viewpoint

As we have been discussing throughout this book, we search for evidence: evidence that a crime has in fact been committed; evidence of when the crime was committed and who committed it; evidence suggesting why the crime was committed (motive). At trial, the judge or jury determines guilt or innocence of the accused based on the evidence presented. In a broad sense, **evidence** is anything allowed by a judge to be presented in court to prove whether the question or issue is true or not.

Evidence is categorized as **real evidence**—any physical object such as a gun; **demonstrative evidence**—a sketch or drawing of a crime scene; or **testimonial evidence**—oral testimony from a witness, officer or others testifying in court. Sometimes evidence may comprise all three: real, demonstrative and testimonial. An example would be a lab technician testifying that the laboratory analysis of a "green plant-like substance" submitted to the lab by the police was in fact cannabis sativa—marijuana.

Evidence is further classified as being either direct or circumstantial. **Direct evidence** either proves or disproves a fact at issue. An identifiable fingerprint left on a gun is either the suspect's or it isn't. In most cases, direct evidence is testimony as to information gathered from a person's senses about what they saw, heard or smelled.

Circumstantial evidence is indirect proof from which facts may be drawn. It's based on an ***inference***: a process of reasoning from which a fact or facts can be deduced. A suspect's blood submitted to DNA analysis proving he or she was at a crime scene doesn't prove the suspect committed the crime, but it may be ***circumstantial evidence*** of guilt. ***Real evidence*** is often given more weight in court because it's not affected by human emotion or perception. ***Weight*** deals with how believable the evidence is to the jury. For example, a fingerprint either belongs to a specific person, or it doesn't.

Evidence gets even more complicated. In the court arena, evidence is further classified as being relevant, material or competent. ***Relevant evidence*** either proves or disproves a fact at issue and whether or not there is a connection between the evidence being offered and the issue to be proven or not proven. Does the evidence have to do with the issues in the case being tried? For example, in states that don't have the rape shield law, you may have a defense attorney arguing in court that the past sexual history of the victim of a rape is *irrelevant* to the issue being raised by the prosecutor. This is a matter the judge would rule on to determine whether the victim's past sexual history was *relevant* to the facts at issue in the case. Many of the rules of evidence are designed to prevent a jury from hearing or seeing improper evidence.

Material evidence refers to whether or not a specific type of evidence will assist in proving an issue raised in court. Would its omission affect the outcome of the case? For example, defense arguments that fingerprints are not a scientific method of proving the identity of a person would likely be ruled as being ***immaterial*** because fingerprint identification has long been accepted in court. In order for evidence to be *competent*, and thus admissible in court, it must have been legally obtained.

Chapter Two Endnotes

1. Brian A. Reaves and Timothy C. Hart. Law Enforcement Management and Administration Statistics, 1994, Washington D.C., Bureau of Justice, 2000

2. Criminal Investigation, Second Edition, Ronald F. Becker, Jones and Bartlett Publishers, Boston, 2005.

3. Criminalistics, An Introduction to Forensic Science, 8th Edition, by Richard Saferstein, Prentice Hall, New Jersey, 2004.

4. Osterburg, James & Ward, Richard, Criminal Investigation-A Method for Reconstructing the Past, 2nd Edition, Anderson Publishing, Cincinnati, Ohio, 1977, p.74

5. Criminal Investigation, Swanson, Chamelin, Territo, & Taylor McGraw Hill, 2006. Page 302

6. Criminal Investigation, Second Edition, Ronald F. Becker, Jones and Bartlett Publishers, Boston, 2005., p.123

7. Osterburg, James & Ward, Richard, Criminal Investigation-A Method for Reconstructing the Past, 2nd Edition, Anderson Publishing, Cincinnati, Ohio, 1977, p.631

Chapter Three

Murder

Nothing grabs the attention of the public like a murder. It is the most serious statutory crime. When a life is taken by another person, the act is subject to a great deal of scrutiny by the media, often making front-page news. According the Federal Bureau of Investigation Uniform Crime Report (1975-2001), there are approximately 15,000 murders reported in the United States each year. Most occur in large cities.

The most commonly used weapon is a firearm. About a third of the victims are between the ages of 20 and 29. Blacks are victims of murder more often than whites. In the vast majority of cases (80%), there was a relationship between the killer and the victim.[1]

People sometimes get confused between the terms *homicide* and *murder*. A **homicide** is the intentional, but lawful, killing of one person by another, for example, when the state executes a prisoner or a police officer lawfully shoots and kills a suspect. Death at the hands of another in these cases is considered to be **justifiable homicide** and non-criminal.

Murder is the most serious statutory crime.
Photo Courtesy of Tri-Tech, Inc.

The definitions for **murder** vary from state to state, but all share common elements. For the purposes of this text, murder is defined as "intentionally causing the death of another through force, suicide, duress, or deception." Many states further classify murder into first-, second- or third-degree, while others use legal terms such as **capital felony**, which refers to the murder of a police officer or other law enforcement official, murder by hire, murder committed in the commission of a felony, murder committed by a kidnapper, and so on. Other categories of murder include various degrees of **manslaughter**. Regardless of the legal category, the common element in the most serious category of murder is **intent** which is often referred to as premeditation. **Premeditation** means advance planning or preparation, regardless of how brief that planning may have been.

Cause of Death

In Chapter One we discussed the legal significance of establishing the cause of death. Death may result from a criminal act, a suicide or natural causes. Ultimately, the pathologist performing an autopsy determines the cause of death. But in cases in which a criminal act is suspected, but not obvious, the details of the autopsy can greatly assist an investigator in reconstructing how the crime occurred.

Death may result from a criminal act - or from a suicide.
Photo Courtesy of Tri-Tech, Inc.

Estimating the Time of Death

The condition of the victim's body can yield a wealth of information to an experienced investigator. Obviously, if there are credible witnesses to the crime, it is simple to determine the time the murder occurred. When witnesses are not present and the victim's body is found by another person, a host of variables presents itself, which may mean that the time of death becomes a vital aspect of the investigation.

Why? Because someone killed another person. When we eventually question a suspect(s), we look for flaws in their alibis—where do they say they were when the victim was killed? Could the person have been at the scene? Or a decomposed body is found partially buried in the woods or another location, and it's important to know whether it's been months or years since the crime occurred.

Although a forensic pathologist provides the best estimate of the time of death, it may take days or weeks to determine. The investigator can make a fairly accurate on-scene estimate based on rigor mortis and body temperature.

Rigor Mortis

Rigor means "stiff," and *mortis* is Latin for "dead." Sometimes you hear old-time detectives using wry humor, for example, saying, "There are two *stiffs* upstairs."

So **rigor mortis** is the natural stiffening of the body after death. The bones of the body are not what become stiff; they are already hard. When death occurs, the muscles in the body relax (flaccidity), then become rigid. It's the muscles tissue that becomes stiff because of a breakdown of amino acids and other chemical changes. Under most conditions, rigor mortis appears within two to four hours in the jaw and hands and four to six hours in the larger muscles of the body.

Rigor becomes fully developed within 12 hours after death. Rigor mortis disappears in the same order it appeared, from the jaw and facial area to the larger muscles, then the full body.

Cold slows down the rate of rigor, and heat speeds it up. The very young and the very old have reduced amounts of rigor mortis.

Body Temperature

Many factors affect the cooling rate of a body, which maintains a 98-degree Fahrenheit constant temperature in life, regardless of weather or clothing. After death, the body cools to the approximate temperature of its surrounding environment. However, the rate at which this occurs is affected by how the body is clothed, the surface the body is resting on, how large or obese the person is, whether or not the body was covered, etc.

Given normal conditions, the body loses heat at a rate of about 1.5 degrees F per hour. A rectal thermometer can be used to make this determination, but this may not be practical at a crime scene. However, if the armpits are warm to the touch, it's likely that death has occurred within the past several hours. If the overall body is cool and clammy, then a good estimate of the time of death is between 12 and 24 hours. Rigor mortis and body temperature used in conjunction provide an investigator with a good "best guess" estimate of when a person was killed.

Postmortem Lividity

When death occurs, the heart stops pumping, and the blood stops circulating. Gravity forces the blood to the lowest level of the body. This causes discoloration in the lower extremities, called *lividity stains*, which appear dark blue or purple.

Postmortem lividity patterns can indicate both approximate time of death and whether a body was moved. If the body is on its back, lividity will appear on the lower portion of the back and legs. If the body is on its front, lividity will appear on the chest, legs, and stomach. Also known as *livor mortis*, postmortem lividity begins approximately thirty minutes to three hours after death and is fully apparent within four to five hours. Body parts compressed against a surface will not display lividity stains because blood is prevented from entering that area after death. Because of the clotting of the blood, even if the body is moved, lividity stains will be visible where they began. The color of the skin may indicate the cause of death: carbon monoxide poisoning, for example, results in a cherry-red color, while carbon dioxide poisoning creates a blue tinge on the skin.

Stomach Contents

During an autopsy, the stomach contents of the deceased are examined. This assists the investigator in determining how long before death the deceased ate. Digestion can be fairly accurately estimated, so a pathologist can usually determine how long the victim lived after eating.

Decomposition of the Body

The longer it takes for a body to be discovered, the more difficult it becomes to establish an accurate time of death. After death, the gases in the stomach (methane) cause distension in both the stomach and abdomen. The higher the temperature, the higher the rate of decomposition. The lower the temperature, the lower the rate of decomposition. The body becomes ***adipocerous***, meaning that a waxy, soapy appearance develops within three months of death, depending on the environmental temperature.

Outdoor Crime Scene and Skeletal Remains

Who is the victim? How did he/she die? Who killed him/her? Outdoor murder investigations and those in which death and decomposition occurred long ago pose special problems. Clothing, jewelry, and/or identification may not be present. There may not be obvious trauma, such as a hole in the skull. The bones, body parts and other physical evidence may have been scattered over large sections of terrain by the criminal or by animals.

We approach these types of crime scenes as though we were going on an archeological dig. A determination must be made of what can reasonably be concluded about the boundaries of the scene of the crime and which types of forensic specialization might be needed. This needs to be done before the area can be properly secured, the evidence can be identified and collected, and reconstruction of the scene can begin.

It is incumbent on the lead investigator to form an investigative recovery team from a variety of scientific fields. In addition to the medical examiner, such a team would consist of ***evidence technicians*** to identify, collect, preserve and record physical evidence; a ***forensic anthropologist*** for body identification and reconstruction; a ***forensic entomologist*** to use insect identification to determine approximate time of death; a ***forensic odontologist*** for dental identification; and ***lab personnel***, who can collect DNA from bone marrow.

Forensic Anthropology

If all that remains of the body is a skeleton, a forensic anthropologist can help determine answers to the following questions:

- *Are the remains human?*

- *Is the skeleton of a male or female?*

- *Approximate age?*

- *Approximate height?*

- *Ethnic origin?*

- *Evidence of a homicide?*

Forensic Entomology

Different types of insects are present in the human body during the various stages of decomposition. Fly larvae feed on decomposing tissues and represent the earliest stages of decomposition. In Katherine Steck-Flynn's 2003 Article "The Role of Entomology in Forensic Investigation," the author describes the value of insects in investigating cases of skeletal remains. Flynn points out that "soil-dwelling" insects exist only in the skeletal stage. If a body is found outdoors, soil samples must be taken from underneath it and up to three feet from it.[2]

The *forensic entomologist* (a scientist who applies the study of insects to legal issues) can estimate the length of time a body has been in the soil by examining the insect life in and around the body. Insects can prove very useful in determining whether the body has decomposed in the location where it is found and whether the body might have been transported after death.

Forensic Dentistry

A *forensic odontologist* is a dentist who has received special training. He or she may be able to identify the body by comparing skeletal teeth with dental records. Like fingerprints, no two sets of human teeth are identical. "On the basis of skull and jaw formation, a forensic dentist may be able to give investigators valuable opinions and information as to the victim's age, race, sex and, possibly, unusual habits."[3]

Identification pre-supposes that the police have an idea who the person is and can obtain dental records with which to make a comparison.

Specialization: Formation of a Recovery Team

When we get into the highly specialized areas of forensic anthropology, forensic dentistry and forensic entomology, neither an investigator nor department personnel responsible for processing a crime scene are expected to have a thorough knowledge of how to collect these types of evidence. Because of the extraordinary investigative problems encountered with skeletal remains, the skilled investigator should recognize the need to include experts from a wide range of scientific fields in a recovery team at the earliest possible stages of the investigation.

In addition to the medical examiner, such a team would consist of evidence technicians to record the crime scene and recognize, collect, and preserve physical evidence; a forensic anthropologist for body identification and reconstruction; a forensic entomologist for insect identification, to determine approximate time of death; a forensic odontologist to determine dental evidence; and forensic laboratory personnel to collect DNA and other probative evidence.

The medical examiner and evidence technicians will probably be employees of local or state governments and readily available to the investigator. Because the majority of homicide investigations don't require the services of a forensic anthropologist, forensic entomologist, or forensic dentist, it would be unusual for them to be on the staff of a police department, or even readily available to be called on a moment's notice. It's up to the investigator to recruit, retain and motivate scientists who want to become involved in these types of cases and are willing to do so for little or no money.

Recruiting and Retaining an Investigative Team

How do you, as an investigator, locate, recruit, and retain scientists? Start by asking your local medical examiner and evidence technicians for names of experts in forensic anthropology, dentistry and entomology. Contact the FBI Crime Laboratory—still the oldest and most respected forensic experts in the world—for assistance and/or references to experts in your area.

Use the Internet. Type in any of the above key words, and you will find a host of organizations, such as the American Board of Forensic Odontology, and people who are experts in the above areas. Fine-tune your search for your state and locality.

Make a list. Don't be surprised if your local college or university has a professor on staff who has been studying entomology for many years or a dental school with a professor who specializes in reconstructive dentistry. Many people watch *CSI* and *Law & Order*, and the mystique of working with the police on these types of cases will work to your advantage.

You need to make them feel important. Visit them at their place of work so they can tell their colleagues the police are asking for their help. Buy them lunch. Provide them with a police identification card that says "Police Forensic Expert," and give them a miniature badge to carry in their wallets.

Provide them with a tour of the station and introduce them to the chief. Invite them to provide in-service or police academy training in their area of specialization. Give them a special police decal for their car. When they do show up at a crime scene, stop everything and accommodate show up at a crime scene, stop everything and accommodate them. Make it a big deal they are there. Send letters of commendation for their services. Invite them to police awards ceremonies. Stay in touch with them even when their services aren't needed. Most of these things don't cost a dime, but you'll be surprised what people are willing to do if they believe their service is appreciated.

The Autopsy

Once all of the evidence from the scene has been recorded and collected and evidence integrity is established by maintaining the chain of custody, the skeletal remains are removed to the morgue for examination by the medical examiner/forensic pathologist for autopsy. The term *autopsy* is derived from the Greek and means "to see for yourself." An autopsy, also known as a *post-mortem examination*, is a medical procedure conducted to determine the cause, manner and circumstances of a person's death.

In the case of skeletal remains, the assistance of all members of the investigative team may be needed to reconstruct what happened. Obviously, a decomposed body found buried in the woods or elsewhere is highly suspicious,

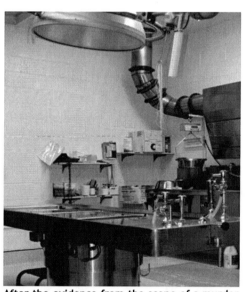

After the evidence from the scene of a murder has been collected, the skeletal remains are removed to the morgue for examination by autopsy. *Photo Courtesy of Tri-Tech, Inc.*

but if no unnatural cause of death is found, can the investigator prove that a crime exists? Decomposition begins at death, and rates of decomposition vary greatly depending on environmental conditions. The recovery team can greatly assist an investigator in determining the cause of death and provide information vital to an on-going investigation.

Motive

Motive and other information about a crime can sometimes be discovered by lifting impressions from paper that lay beneath an original handwritten document.   Courtesy of BVDA International

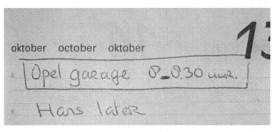

Motive and opportunity are key elements in any criminal investigation. One of the reasons we spend so much time on the question of when a person died is to be able to determine whether a particular suspect the opportunity to commit the crime. An alibi is tied to time and place. Could the suspect have been at the scene of the crime at the right time?

Why people commit the crime of murder is often difficult to determine. Motive is closely associated with *intent* and provides the investigator with a lead as to who had a reason to kill the victim.

Since Cain slew Abel, the reasons people kill one another have been as numerous as the grains of sand at the beach. However, an old police saying is "follow the money." Determining who would gain from the victim's death (by examining estates, wills, insurance, etc.) has led to the solving of countless murder cases.

Although the list is endless, some of the more common motives for murder are those with sexual connotations, jealousy, rage, revenge, silencing a person who has incriminating information, and blackmail.

Putting it all Together

The following exercise places many of the major topics we have been discussing into a real-life scenario.

Read the following case and answer the questions that follow:

> The superintendent of an apartment building is concerned about an elderly resident he hasn't seen in several days. He goes to her second-floor apartment and observes that the front door is slightly open. After calling out and receiving no response, he enters the apartment and finds the elderly woman in her bedroom lying on the bed. He approaches, observes she is not moving, and sees what appears to be a pool of blood

in the bed next to her head. He sees a gun on the floor near the bed. He rushes out and calls the police.

Two police officers—the officer who patrols the area in which the address is located and another patrol unit from an adjoining area—are sent to the scene by the police dispatcher. The area sergeant hears the call on the radio and, since a death may be involved, decides to respond.

The arriving officers meet the superintendent in the hallway adjacent to the apartment and interview him as to what he did and observed. He repeats his story about not having seen the elderly woman for several days, adds that her name is Delores Jefferson and that her mail has been piling up in the mailbox of the foyer to the apartment building. He tells the officers about finding the door partially open and going in to see whether Mrs. Jefferson was okay. He adds that he is a World War II veteran and knows a dead body when he sees it, that he found Mrs. Jefferson dead in the bedroom and saw a pool of blood on the bed next to her head and a gun on the floor, that he "didn't touch nothing," and that he called the police.

Upon entering the apartment, the officers go into the bedroom and see a woman, who appears to be approximately 80 years of age, clothed in a nightgown and lying on her back on the bed. The officers note that there is a bullet entry wound to her head. There is considerable tattooing and tearing of the skin surrounding the entry wound and a pool of blood on the bed next to her head. She has no pulse, and rigor mortis is fully developed. There is a .38 caliber revolver on the floor next to the bed. There is no one else in the apartment. Death is certain, but the responding officers don't know whether it is a suicide or a murder.

A short time later, two detectives from the department's Crimes Against Persons Division arrive at the scene. The detectives do a walk-through of the crime scene and note the following: the .38-caliber revolver is loaded with five bullets and one spent cartridge casing; the woman has a blunt-force wound to the back of her head; she has a bullet entry and exit wound to her head with considerable tattooing and tearing of the skin surrounding the entry wound; a bullet hole is located in a wall next to the bed, underneath a window, where a single spent bullet is later recovered; what appears to be blood is present on the bed and floor next to the bed; rigor mortis is fully developed; postmortem lividity is readily apparent on the front of the woman's body; an electrical cord is wound around the woman's neck; a ligature wound is evident to the neck with signs of bruising and blood congestion just above and below the furrow caused by the ligature; what appears to be blood spatter is located in the bathroom.

Investigative Questions

Question #1:   *Based on the information contained in the reading section, what would be the most important steps for the officer arriving first at the scene to take?*

Question #2:   *Applying the "exigent circumstances" exception to the search warrant rule, at which point should the police obtain a search warrant?*

Question #3:   *What can reasonably be concluded based on the information relative to the electrical cord and ligature wound around the woman's neck?*

Question #4:   *Because considerable tattooing and tearing of the skin was found on the woman's head at the location of the bullet entrance wound, what is most likely to have occurred?*

Question #5:   *If the spent bullet recovered in the wall didn't match the .38-caliber revolver found on the floor next to the bed, what is most logically indicated?*

Question #6:   *Based on the information provided, it's most likely that the woman's time of death was at least how long ago?*

Question #7:   *What can most logically be deduced from the information relative to postmortem lividity of the woman's body?*

Question #8:   *A laboratory test determines that the blood found by the bed was of the same blood type as that of the victim. However, the blood found in the bathroom is a different blood type than that of the victim. Based on these facts, what can most logically be concluded?*

Answers to Investigative Questions

Answer #1:   Determine whether a suspect(s) is still in the apartment. Protect the crime scene. Notify headquarters via land line or cell phone of the situation.

Answer #2:   The exigent circumstances exception to the search warrant rule does not include a "murder scene exception" (Mincey v. Arizona, 437, U.S. 385 [1978]). Police may enter a murder scene without a warrant in order to render immediate aid, search for other victims or the killer, and preserve and collect perishable evidence in plain view. A search and seizure warrant must then be obtained.

Answer #3:   A horizontal groove or furrow cut by a ligature is often visible on the throat and normally is about the width of the ligature. Signs of bruising and blood congestion just above and below the furrow indicate the victim was alive when it was applied.

Answer #4:   The contact wound indicates that a firearm was fired while in contact with the skin or up to a distance of two or three inches from the body. (The tearing of the tissue surrounding a contact wound results when gases that entering the wound seek to reverse direction and escape.)

Answer #5:   If the bullet from the wall didn't match the weapon at the scene, then it wasn't fired from that weapon.

Answer #6:   Rigor mortis is evident at first in the small muscles of the hands and jaw in two to four hours. It becomes obvious in the larger muscles in four to six hours, and it is fully developed in twelve hours. The woman has been dead for at least twelve hours.

Answer #7:   Postmortem lividity is the medical term describing the bluish-purple color that develops after death in the lowest part of the body. Because the woman was found lying on her back, postmortem lividity was present on the front of her body, it can reasonably be concluded the woman's body was moved after death.

Answer #8:   The blood found in the bathroom was not that of the victim and could possibly be that of a suspect.

Chapter Three Endnotes

1. Federal Bureau of Investigation Uniform Crime Report (1975-2001).

2. Criminal Investigation, Swanson, Charles, Chamelin, Neil, and Territo, Leonard: 7th Edition, McGraw Hill, 2000, pg. 94.

3. "The Role of Entomology in Forensic Investigation." Katherine Steck-Flynn, 2003, http://www.crimeandclues.com/ entomology_intro.htm

Chapter Four

Rape

Definition

With the exception of murder, many consider forcible rape the most serous crime a person can commit. Physical evidence plays a key role in investigating the crime of rape because of its unique nature and the crucial role of physical evidence in obtaining a conviction. Definitions of what constitute rape differ at the federal, state, and local levels. For the purposes of this book, *rape* is defined as *sexual intercourse against a person's will by force or threat of force.*

Forcible rape—the term used to classify rape from other sexual crimes—is the only sex offense that is an index crime listed in the Federal Bureau of Investigation's Uniform Crime Report. Although rape is usually thought of as a gender-specific crime, the number of reported rapes among persons of the same sex is steadily rising.

A strong force in the under-reporting of the crime is social stigma. Studies indicate that rape is substantially under-reported when it involves persons of the same gender. Many states now use the term *sexual assault* rather than rape in order to differentiate between a variety of legal variables regarding severity of punishment and the significance of the physical and psychological threat to the victim and/or the public. These factors may include the age of the victim, the age of the perpetrator, mental incapacitation, ability under the law to give consent, use or threat of a weapon, physical injury to the victim, spousal or other legal relationship, and so on.

In many jurisdictions, sexual assault is divided into a series of graded offenses depending on the perceived legal seriousness of the crime and aggravating conditions. These offenses may range from Sexual Assault in the First Degree through Sexual Assault in the Fourth Degree.

Establishing the *corpus delicti*—that a criminal act has in fact occurred—is more complex in rape cases than in other serious crimes because of the significant physical and psychological impact to the victim, as well as prevailing social attitudes. Investigators must establish that the *elements of the crime*, or factors that must occur for an act to be considered a type of crime be proven under the court standard of *proof beyond a reasonable doubt*, not just probable cause. Whether or not consent was present or forensic evidence can link a suspect to the crime scene and/or victim may become the focal point of the case.

Scope of the Crime — Why Rape is not Reported to the Police

The Uniform Crime Report reveals that 94,635 persons were raped in the United States in 2004. These figures represent *reported* forcible rapes, not the number of people who were *actually* raped. Most experts agree that forcible rape often goes unreported. Although we don't have reliable figures of how many people are raped each year, according to a 1999 FBI Law Enforcement Bulletin, up to 84% of all sexual assaults go unreported.[1]

Women sometimes do not report rapes because they have worries about unsympathetic treatment by the police or do not believe the police will be able to apprehend the suspect.   Photo Courtesy of Tri-Tech, Inc.

A recently published textbook on criminal investigation cites a series of studies indicating why women do not report being raped.

Why women do not report being raped:

1. Worries of unsympathetic treatment from police and discomforting procedures.

2. Lack of belief in the ability of the police to apprehend the suspect.

3. Apprehension of being further victimized by court proceedings as a result of seeing other victims endure such treatment on television programs or in newspaper reports.

4. Embarrassment about publicity, however limited.

5. Fear of reprisal by the rapist.[2]

Other textbooks on criminal investigation posit that perceived ill treatment by law enforcement officers is the main reason rape is not reported. Although this may be true in isolated instances, in my 30 years of investigative experience, I have found that police officers grasp the psychological trauma experienced by rape victims and go to great lengths to treat the victim with compassion and professionalism.

Initial Contact With the Rape Victim

Most police administrators plan police assignments under the theory of *police omnipresence*—the police are everywhere, and if you commit a crime you will be apprehended rapidly. The latest trend in *computer-aided dispatching (CAD)* is a patrol strategy that concentrates on the prevention of crime and rapid response if it does occur. However, according to recent Bureau of Justice statistics, almost 80% of forcible rapes occur in an indoor location, and there is some relationship between victim and offender. So police patrol is not likely to prevent a rape from being committed.

From a law enforcement perspective, we want to arrest the perpetrator quickly, using investigative techniques that ensure a conviction and also a process that causes the least amount of psychological trauma to the victim. It's more likely than not that this will begin with a call from the victim to the police. How this initial contact is handled, often by civilian dispatchers or other communications personnel, is critical.

Depending on the variables presented in the initial contact, police administrators should insure that personnel are trained to do the following:

- Ask the victim whether she sustained serious physical injury and is in need of immediate medical assistance. If so, dispatch an ambulance.

- Ask the victim whether she can identify or describe the suspect. Follow protocol relative to providing this information to patrol units.

- Immediately dispatch a patrol unit to the scene.

- Tell the victim to wait for the police to arrive if she is in a safe location.

- Instruct the victim not to alter her physical appearance or touch anything at the scene.

- Advise the victim not to wash or douche before having a medical examination.[3]

It's the natural instinct of the victim of a rape to wash, douche, change clothing, or use other self-help mechanisms. First-contact personnel (beginning with the police dispatcher or police complaint receiver) should do everything possible to ensure the victim doesn't do these things.

In addition to the location where the rape actually took place (or, in the case of an abduction, the points of contact and release), the *victim* is the crime scene.

Although most forcible rape cases are legitimate and investigators should proceed under that assumption, investigators do have a responsibility to those falsely accused. We can best fulfill this responsibility by conducting a thorough investigation. Unlike with many other crimes, convictions in rape cases may require corroborative evidence other than just the victim's testimony in court.

First Responders

As with any other crime of violence, the primary responsibility of the first officer arriving at the scene is to ensure the victim receives medical attention. It's crucial that the victim be bought to a hospital so that a physical examination can be conducted to establish the crime of rape or sexual assault. Because the clothing of the victim will be taken as evidence, a change of clothing should be brought to the hospital whenever possible. Maintaining the chain of evidence is paramount, and a police officer, preferably female, should accompany the victim in the ambulance.

In addition to following normal procedures in protecting primary and secondary crime scenes, a preliminary interview with the victim (preferably by a female officer) should be conducted in private to determine whether she knows or can identify the person who raped her. A physical description of the rapist should be obtained and the victim should be asked to explain what happened. A detailed follow-up interview should be conducted by the investigator, a trained rape counselor or other care provider in a setting most comfortable to the victim. The responsibility of first responders to protect the scene(s) of the crime and isolate and detain any witnesses is crucial.

Goals of a Search of the Crime Scene

As we previously discussed, the crime scene encompasses all areas in which people connected with a crime are located shortly before and after the crime. Both the perpetrator and the victim moved through physical locations in order for the crime to be committed, while the crime was committed, and after the crime was committed. In searching a crime scene we operate under the premise that whenever human beings interact with any inanimate or animate object, something is either taken away or left behind.

The objectives of the search of a crime scene in a forcible rape case are the same as in any other major case.

We want to accomplish the following:

1. *Reconstruct what happened and establish that a crime occurred.*

2. *Identify, document, and collect evidence of what occurred.*

3. *Link the victim and the suspect to the scene of the crime.*

4. *Identify and locate any witnesses.*

5. *Identify and apprehend the person(s) who committed the crime.*

Identification and Collection of Rape Evidence

Physical evidence is *anything tangible that can establish that a crime has been committed or link the crime and the victim and/or the perpetrator to the victim.* However, before physical evidence can be collected it, **must first be recognized** as such by the investigator. Even if evidence is recognized, unless it is properly collected, preserved, and analyzed, its value will be limited in court.

Although many departments have specialized personnel to process crime scenes, all police officers should have a thorough knowledge of the forensic capabilities of the crime laboratory and the importance of securing and collecting evidence. While there is no substitute for training and experience, the collection and preservation of crime scene evidence isn't just the purview of evidence technicians and detectives. Except in very complex cases, the average police officer is capable of reconstructing the scene of the crime and conducting a systematic search for evidence.

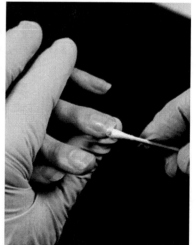

Fingernail scrapings can be used to collect an attacker's DNA.
Photo Courtesy of Tri-Tech, Inc.

Unless it's a stranger-to-stranger rape case, there are often claims by the perpetrator that intercourse was consensual. Absent any evidence to the contrary, it becomes the victim's word against that of the perpetrator. So any sign of a struggle at the scene (broken furniture or other objects, items in disarray, etc.) should be photographed and videotaped. Photographs of the injuries are usually taken at the hospital. The bedding or any other object on which the rape took place should be preserved and sent to the crime lab for analysis.

The contact between the victim and the perpetrator may have resulted in the transfer of physical evidence in the form of semen, blood, hairs, skin, fibers, or other trace evidence. This will be vital in identifying the assailant and/or prosecuting the case. All such evidence needs to be properly collected, including the clothing and undergarments worn by the victim. Evidence technicians can examine the evidence using oblique and ultraviolet light to help spot hair and fibers and blue light to assist in detecting semen.

The disconnect between books on forensic science and real-life investigations is the books' suggestion that the victim should be asked to disrobe over a clean cloth or bed sheet so that any fibers or loose pubic hairs from the perpetrator can be properly collected and later analyzed at the laboratory. In an ideal world, this would be a perfect way to collect this type of evidence. However, only in the mind of the scientist or academician do rapes occur in a sterile environment conducive to this type of evidence collection. Although most rapes do occur inside, they may take place in the stairway of large apartment building, the bathroom of a bar or nightclub, inside a vehicle, or at another location not conducive to this type of evidence gathering.

Whether the victim is lying in a traumatized fetal ball suffering from shock or otherwise injured from her attacker, our first responsibility to provide the victim with medical attention at a hospital. Even if the victim were able to disrobe at the scene, this would have to be done by a female police officer. Because female officers only make up about 12% of police forces nationally, even large cities may not have a female officer readily available to provide this type of evidence collection. In the majority of cases, the search of the victim's clothing for evidence of the crime is done at the hospital. This is often a better setting in which to have the victim disrobe, photograph any injuries, and preserve evidence by placing each article of clothing in a separate container for later lab analysis.

Again, because the chain of custody of evidence is vital, a police officer must accompany the victim to the hospital, which often means an officer needs to ride in the ambulance with the victim.

The Medical Examination

Physical evidence of a sexual assault must be properly collected. Photo Courtesy of Tri-Tech, Inc.

Even if your department has personnel who specialize in investigating the crime of rape, not every hospital is equal when it comes to the type of medical examination required. Large cities often have hospitals staffed with medical personnel who receive specialized training in the physical examination required. They also often have rape counselors and psychological services available for victims. Smaller communities may have only one hospital and may not be able to provide the same level of service. In a big city or a small town, the fact remains that doctors are not usually in the business of evidence collection. Although victim *rape collection kits* are standard at almost every medical facility, this doesn't mean that evidence will be collected properly.

It's the responsibility of those in charge of the department's investigative function to ensure there is a proper liaison between the department and the city's or town's hospital(s). This means meeting with doctors and staff and explaining the legal nuances of why the evidence is necessary and the information such evidence can provide. Hospital staff meetings would be a perfect time for both the police and members of the medical profession to discuss not only how rape cases will be handled, but how the chain of custody of evidence can be preserved.

The following types of physical evidence are collected during the medical examination for laboratory analysis:

Evidence	Use
Hair (Both pubic hair and head hair)	Cannot individually identify a person unless the root is present.
	Does provide strong collaborative evidence individual was at the crime.
	Can be distinguished between human and animal. Race may be able to be determined. May be able to establish the part of the body from which hair came from.
Blood	Can be distinguished between human and animal. DNA analysis can provide individual identification.
Fingernail Scrapings	To collect DNA evidence for individual analysis and identification.
Vaginal Swabs and Smear	To collect DNA evidence for individual analysis and identification.
Rectal Swabs and Smear	To collect DNA evidence for individual analysis and identification.
Oral Swabs and Smear	To collect DNA evidence for individual analysis and identification.

The preceding types of evidence are most useful in cases in which the perpetrator unknown to the to victim. However, even if the victim's assailant is known and an arrest is made shortly after the crime based on probable cause, it's still critical that all evidence protocols described in this book be followed.

Arrest requires only probable cause. A much higher standard—that of proof beyond a reasonable doubt—is needed for conviction in court. Experienced investigators know that the variables under which an arrest is initially made can change—the evidence doesn't support the initial claims of the victim or witnesses; people change their versions of what they initially say occurred; the perpetrator claims the sex was consensual, and so on. Our system of justice relies heavily on tangible (real) evidence because it's not affected by emotion or perception, and logical conclusions can be drawn from the science supporting what the evidence represents.

Physical Injury to the Victim

Any physical injury to the victim, such as bruises and bleeding, must be photographed. Biological evidence, such as semen, may indicate that sexual intercourse took place, but it doesn't establish a *prima facie* case of rape. Injury to the victim is corroborative evidence of violence and especially useful in cases in which the suspect is claiming consensual sex.

Deoxyribonucleic Acid (DNA)

The discovery of DNA has revolutionized criminal investigation. An individual's identity can be obtained from sweat, skin, blood, tissue, hair, semen, mucus, saliva, or almost any biological sample. The evidence collected at the crime scene and during the medical examination of the victim is crucial to obtaining DNA evidence that may identify the perpetrator. If there is a suspect in the case, there are several ways a DNA sample can be obtained: voluntarily, surreptitiously, or under court order as a result of a search warrant. I prefer a search warrant because, even with a signed authorization from the suspect indicating *knowing and intelligent consent*, or a legal search through a person's trash for a discarded napkin containing saliva, these methods are fraught with legal challenges.

Voluntary Submission of a DNA Sample

People cannot be forced to provide a sample of their DNA. A signed and witnessed authorization form from the suspect must be obtained. The form contains similar language to the waiver of Miranda rights form all police officers are familiar with. It includes consent to an oral swab and/or a blood sample for the purposes of DNA testing. Having a suspect use a cotton swab to rub the inside of his mouth (cheek) is a simple procedure any police officer can perform.

Surreptitiously Obtaining a Suspect's DNA

Because DNA can be obtained from biological material, anything containing saliva, mucus, skin, etc., may be used to get a DNA typing of an individual. The key is that the suspect must have discarded an item, such as a cigarette butt, in a public place the police legally have access to. A soda can, food, or a napkin may have skin cells or saliva that could result in a DNA typing linking the suspect to the rape.

Search Warrant

Because a search warrant must be specific as to the evidence sought, anything from which a DNA analysis can be obtained must be listed. This would include clothing worn by the suspect, bloodstains, anywhere semen stains might exist, etc. In the case of clothing worn by the suspect, it must be legally obtained. If the suspect is under arrest, one could theoretically seize the clothing without a warrant. However, as mentioned earlier, a search and seizure warrant is the preferred method of obtaining DNA evidence because the likelihood of such evidence being admitted in court is substantially greater than when the suspect either voluntary submits evidence or it is obtained in a surreptitious manner or as part of a search incidental to arrest.

The Combined DNA Index System (CODIS)

In cases in which the rapist isn't known to the victim, DNA typing of biological material recovered from the crime scene and/or victim can be submitted to the Federal Bureau of Investigation's database of DNA profiles of convicted offenders, unsolved crime scenes, and missing persons. All states have now mandated the collection of DNA samples of convicted rapists. This tool allows crime laboratories to electronically compare DNA profiles from those developed in the investigation to those in a national database.

Chapter Four Endnotes

1. Federal Bureau of Investigation, Law Enforcement Bulletin, (1999).

2. Criminal Investigation, sixth Edition, Wayne W. Bennett and Karen M. Hess, Wadsworth/Thomson Learning, 2002

3. Criminal Investigation, Ninth Edition, Charles Swanson, Neil Cahmelin, Leonard Territo, and Robert Taylor, McGraw Hill, 2006

Chapter Five

Robbery

Definition

While ***larceny*** is defined as the *taking of tangible personal property of another by trespass,* **robbery** is *larceny by force or threat of force.* Robbery is the face-to-face meeting of the victim and perpetrator and the potential for or actual violence that makes robbery such a serious crime.

Because of the fear street robbery generates, it has a devastating impact on the quality of life in a community. Although the legal definition of robbery may vary, most states have separated the crime into degrees of legal seriousness depending on a series of variables having to do with the extent or injury or potential threat of injury to the victim(s).

Some of the variables that add to the seriousness of the crime are whether in the course of the robbery a person was injured; whether the robber was armed or indicated he/she was armed; whether the robber was aided by another person; and, in some states, whether the robbery involving the taking of an occupied motor vehicle.

Because force or threat of force is a basic element in the crime of robbery, the investigation must prove the victim was injured, however slightly, or in fear of being injured when the property was taken. When the victim of a robbery suffers serious injury, there is little question that force was used and that the crime is a robbery, not a larceny.

However, in other cases, the difference between larceny and robbery can be subtle.

Consider the following examples:

> A woman is at McDonald's with her small children. She leaves her purse in the booth where they're eating to get some napkins. A thief grabs her purse and runs out the front door. This is a **larceny**—taking the woman's property with the intent to permanently deprive her of that property. No injury or threat was involved.
>
> In the second example, the woman returns to the booth with the napkins just as the perpetrator grabs her purse, and a tug-of-war for the bag ensues. The perpetrator wins and runs out the door with the purse. The woman's wrist has been slightly injured by the tug-of-war. This is a **robbery** instead of a larceny. The perpetrator used force and caused injury in the commission of the crime.

Another example of a **robbery** would be if the perpetrator followed the woman out to her car and said, "Give me your purse, or I'll smash your daughters face in." This is not a larceny because the property was taken by threat of force.

Demographics

According to a 2002 FBI National Crime Victimization Survey, robberies on streets or highways accounted for more than 40% of the robbery offenses in 2001. Robberies of commercial establishments accounted for 26% of the offenses, and robberies in residences made up 12% percent. The remaining robberies occurred in miscellaneous locations.[1]

According to recent victimization studies, only about half of all robberies are reported to the police. Minorities and the poor are more likely to be victims of robbery than others. In almost 90% of robberies, the suspects are male. Most robberies occur in metropolitan areas. Black males tend to be robbed at twice the rate of black females and at two and one-half times the rate of white males.[3] Robbery is usually a stranger-to stranger crime: In about 71% of the cases, the perpetrator and victim do not know each another.

Weapons Used to Commit Robbery

A firearm is used in approximately 40% of robbery cases. Knives or another cutting instrument is used about 8% of the time, and other weapons play a part in 10% of cases. In 42% of robberies, the technique used is of the "strong-arm" type, meaning that no weapon is used. In a strong-arm robbery (mugging), force is usually used—hands, fists, etc.—but no weapon displayed.[2]

Types of Robberies

Street Robberies

About half of all robberies happen on the street.[4] Robberies frequently occur at night in dimly lit areas. The scenario might be a person walking back to his or her car from a restaurant or bar being suddenly confronted by a robber who displays a gun and demands money. Or it could be a purse-snatching or a strong-arm attack at an ATM.

Some robbery victims are confronted by robbers displaying a gun and demanding money. Physical evidence can link the gun to the scene or the victim.   Photo Courtesy of Tri-Tech, Inc.

The crime is often characterized by its quickness and a motive to obtain cash to pay for drugs. Because of the time of day, location, and suddenness of street-level robberies, victims often can't provide more than a basic description of the perpetrator. Even if a suspect is apprehended, absent physical evidence linking the suspect to the scene or victim (for example, if the perpetrator has the victim's credit or ATM card), the victim often can't identify the suspect as the person who robbed him or her.

Convenience Store Robberies

Convenience stores proliferate in our cities and towns, are often open twenty-four hours a day, and do a cash business. They are easy targets because there often is only one employee working, with just a counter separating the robber from ready cash. It's simple for the criminal to case the joint and determine when the business's down times are and whether customers are present or likely to be present in the store. It's also easy to see whether the store has a video surveillance camera and how often police patrols ride by. Even if there is a video camera, a simple mask (ski mask, silk stocking, etc.) can make the perpetrator unidentifiable and escape routes can easily be planned.

Carjackings

A woman is returning to her car with her infant daughter after shopping at a mall. She opens the automobile door and is trying to put the baby in a car seat in the back when she is confronted by four young men who demand the keys to the car and her purse. One backhands her across the face when she doesn't move quickly enough to get the baby out of the car. She is left standing in the parking lot watching her car being driven off.

There are 49,000 carjackings each year, and 8 out of 10 involve a weapon, usually a gun.[5] Ninety-seven percent of offenders are male, and injury results 16% of the time, with serious physical injury resulting in 4% of such offenses.

Carjackings often happen at gas stations, ATMs, car washes, parking lots, shopping centers and convenience stores, restaurants, train stations, and parking control signals.

When I was head of the Narcotics Squad, it wasn't unusual for people from the suburbs who came into a high-crime area late at night to buy coke or dope to have their cars taken by force, leaving them hurt, on foot, alone, and in an area as strange to them as an alien planet.

Investigating Crimes of Robbery

As in the previous chapters, it must be noted that the initial responding officers to a robbery call are not detectives, but patrol officers assigned to the area or an area adjoining the one in which the robbery occurred. The police dispatcher and/or complaint writer receiving the initial call from the victim plays a critical role in obtaining information which may effect the tactics used by officers in responding to the scene.

The following information, *at a minimum*, is what must be gathered:

1. *Is the robbery still in progress?* Cell phones and a variety of alarms have increased the likelihood that a robbery may be reported to the police while still in progress.

2. *What is the exact location where the robbery is occurring or has occurred: a bank, convenience store, parking garage, street, taxicab, home invasion, ATM machine, etc.?* If it's in the past, how long ago did the robbery occur?

3. *Is anyone injured? What is the extent of the injuries? Is an ambulance(s) needed at the scene?*

4. *How many suspects are involved? Was (is) the suspect(s) armed? With what type of weapon: handgun, shotgun, rifle, knife, automatic weapon?*

5. *Is a description of the suspect(s) available?*

6. *Have the suspect(s) left the scene? How? In a car, on foot? What was their direction of travel? If a vehicle was used to escape, what is the description of the vehicle?*

All this information is vital to responding officers. Street-wise cops make it their business to know every business in their assigned areas. They know where every back alley leads and where the closest entrance ramps to the major highways are. If the robbery is in the past, then officers can be positioned at likely escape routes. The MO (method of operation) used by the suspect(s) may provide officers with information to link past robberies and suspects to this robbery. In robbery cases, officers should proceed under the assumption that the suspect is armed, but it's paramount that the police dispatcher relay any information relative to weapons to responding officers. When to use and stop using emergency lights and sirens responding to the call depends largely on the initial information received.

Although medical attention to the injured remains the top priority, responding units should plan and coordinate their efforts prior to arrival at the scene.

Because various types of forensic evidence may be present at the scene of a robbery, the scene should be protected and processed appropriately. Photo Courtesy of Tri-Tech, Inc.

Police scanners are easily purchased, and robbers often post lookouts with cell phones. Street cops often don't use the department's police codes (anyone can figure them out by just listening to a police scanner), but have developed their own codes and language in order to position themselves while responding to and once having arrived at the scene of a crime. "I'll meet you at the Big B," meaning, say, the parking lot of Barney's Big Burgers, is an example of this type of coded language.

If the suspect(s) has already left the scene, it's the responsibility of the first arriving officer to gather pertinent information and advise headquarters so an appropriate radio broadcast can be made giving the information explained in items 1 through 6, above. Because the same type of forensic evidence discussed in previous chapters may be present at the scene of a robbery, the scene should be protected and processed appropriately.

Follow-up Investigations

Depending on the size of the department and other variables, detectives may or may not respond to the scene. As discussed in Chapter Two, patrol officers are certainly capable of handling a robbery investigation. So why should a department have detectives who specialize in robbery investigations?

The question comes down to the best use of patrol resources. Even if a suspect(s) is apprehended at the scene or close by, unless it's a simple purse snatch or street mugging, the work required to put a robbery case together is very time-consuming.

Smaller departments in rural areas with comparatively fewer incidents of crime may be able to have a patrol officer tied up on a robbery investigation for an entire shift, but in a large metropolitan area, where calls for service are stacked and always waiting, patrol officers are needed on the street.

An investigation that is going to take a prolonged period of time (processing the crime scene for evidence, photographs of the scene, written statements, interviews and interrogations, applications for arrest and/or search and seizure warrants, etc.) is a job for a detective. Additionally, detectives who specialize in robbery may recognize a criminal's *modus operandi*. During the investigation, experienced detectives may be able to link a string of robberies together.

Chapter Five Endnotes

1. United States Department of Justice, Federal Bureau of Investigation, 2002 National Crime Victimization Survey (Washington DC. US Printing Office, 2003).

2. Federal Bureau of Investigation, Crime in the United States-1999 Washington DC: Government Printing Office, 2000, p. 28.

3. Criminal Investigation, Osterbury and Ward, page 462)

4. Bureau of Justice Statistics, Criminal Victimization in the United States-1999 Washington DC (Bureau of Justice Statistics, 2000), p.79, table 75.

5. Patsy Klauss, Carjacking in the United States, 1992-1996 (Washington DC: Bureau of Justice Statistics, March 1999).

Chapter Six

Burglary

Definition

According to the FBI's Uniform Crime Reports, **burglary** is *the unlawful entry of a structure to commit a felony or theft, even though no force was used to gain entry.* However, like other serious crimes, burglary is divided into a series of graded offenses and penalties in most states. If the burglar is armed with a deadly weapon or dangerous instrument and/or causes injury to another person, it is considered a very serious crime. A burglar who crawls through a window of a business at 3:00 a.m. and is caught walking out the front door with a computer is committing a serious crime, but it does not rise to the level of the first example. The fear of having someone enter our homes, the loss of an item of great sentimental value, and the invasion of our privacy generate public outrage over the crime of burglary.

According to a 2003 FBI report, a burglary occurs every 14.6 seconds in the United States.[1] Burglary statutes in most states cover unlawful entry into residences, businesses, motor vehicles, aircraft, boats, campers, and ATM and vending machines outside of businesses.

Some burglaries require a high degree of skill and planning, as did the following case I worked on:

WAR STORY

BURGLARY IN PLAIN SIGHT

There is a famous museum in Hartford that displays paintings and other priceless objets d'art. The physical and electronic security are first-rate. Several retired detectives work there as full-time security consultants. Although there is a high degree of public pedestrian traffic through the museum, I couldn't remember the last time anything had been stolen. Then my partner and I got the call to respond to an incident.

When we got to the scene, the museum curator and several security personnel in blue blazers and gray slacks promptly led us to the huge first-floor exhibition hall and pointed to a large wall where a painting by a famous artist was proudly displayed. It was attractively framed and covered the entire wall. I thought it looked very nice. I looked at my partner and he looked back at me and we shrugged our shoulders.

"So, what's the problem?" I asked the curator.

He looked at me incredulously and said, "It's not the right painting. It's a fake. A cheap copy. The original has been stolen!!"

"Stolen. How?"

He raised his eyebrows. "That's what we called you to find out." The curator was embarrassed because the fake painting had hung on the wall for two days before anyone noticed it was a copy.

Apparently, parties unknown had somehow entered the museum, removed the original painting from its frame, replaced it with a replica and put the reproduction back in the original frame.

A couple of hours previously, the curator was leading a group of art students around the main hall when one of the students mentioned the painting was a "good copy." The curator took a closer look and then called the police.

We never did recover the original painting or find out who committed the burglary. Investigation revealed that some pretty sophisticated alarms had been bypassed, and video security cameras had been placed on a continuous loop for four-hour periods.

A high degree of skill is required to bypass alarm codes and reconfigure video surveillance. It would take a team of men to remove the huge painting from the wall, take the frame off, remove the original painting, replace it with a copy in the original frame and re-hang the painting.

Our best lab people came up with nada. My question was, Where do you fence a painting worth half a billion dollars?

My partner and I took a ride to New York City and hooked up with a couple of detectives who had been investigating art crimes for decades The gist of what we learned was that the painting was probably already out of the country and now part of some multi-billionaire's private collection. which meant the buyer would not show the painting to anyone. It was probably in a special underground vault that the buyer visited alone, perhaps enjoying glass of wine while he viewed this and other works of art acquired over the years.

This is the world of rare gems, coins, paintings and sculpture. My partner and I were out of our league and happy to return to investigating murders, rapes and assaults.

Types of Burglars

The Amateur

The average financial loss in residential and commercial burglaries is less than $2,000 in cash or merchandise. The amateur, often working with others, commits burglary as a crime of opportunity with very little pre-planning. The technique used is *smash-and-grab*—ransacking to look for anything of value that can be easily fenced for ready cash, often to support a drug addiction. The type of property taken, such as televisions, costume jewelry, cash, stereos, and other portable objects, typically identifies the work of an amateur burglar, who tends to be younger than the professional burglar.

In 2001, 31% of burglary arrests were of juveniles, with 11.7 percent of those under the age of 15.[2] The amateur burglar is often armed and poses a significant threat of violence to homeowners.

Professional Burglars

Professional burglars tend to be older and engage in a high level of planning prior to committing the crime. The professional frequently gains access without causing obvious damage and doesn't ransack the premises. The property taken is often much more valuable than that taken by the amateur, such as furs, expensive jewelry, negotiable securities and works of art. The victim may not know a burglary has occurred for days or weeks, depending on what was stolen. Professional burglars have developed networks in which to dispose of stolen items.

Conducting Burglary Investigations

This section concentrates on the investigation into burglaries that have already occurred, rather than the tactical approach and response to burglaries in progress. Because a unformed patrol officer(s) is usually the first to respond to the scene of a reported burglary, it's his/her responsibility to ensure the crime scene is protected and prevent residents or business owners from further contaminating it.

The initial investigation determines which items were stolen, serial numbers or individualized marks on each item, whether witnesses or others who may assist in the investigation can be located, etc. It's becoming

Dental stone can be used to preserve tool marks, footprints and tire marks.
Photo Courtesy of Tri-Tech, Inc.

Tire & Footprint Casting Release Spray

CRP LLC

Reorder No. LC-CRS-9

MANUFACTURED BY:
CRIMINAL RESEARCH PRODUCTS, LLP
4719 EXECUTIVE PARK BLVD., SE
SOUTHPORT, NC 28461
800/438-7884

9 oz. Net Wt.

Release spray is used to help separate the casting material from the impression.
Photo Courtesy of Tri-Tech, Inc.

more common to have alarm and video security systems in homes, so investigators will determine whether they are a source of recoverable evidence.

As previously discussed, in smaller departments, the responding officer may be responsible for the entire investigation, but in large departments, detectives who specialize in crimes against property may be assigned to respond to the scene.

The investigation usually begins with determining the point of entry, which may provide information about the suspect(s) as well as about the burglar's direction of approach. This area may be a source of footprints, tire impressions, cigarette butts or other recoverable evidence. The point of entry —window, door, etc.—should be examined for fingerprints and tool marks.

A wide variety of methods are used to gain entry into a premises, ranging from kicking down a door, smashing a window, picking a lock or using a tool to pry open a door, lock or window. As mentioned in Chapter Two, tools such as screwdrivers, tire irons and crowbars leave impressions in objects they come into contact with, usually on window frames and doors through which entry was made. When a burglar inserts a screwdriver or crowbar into the frame of a window or door, some sort of indentation mark, or ***tool mark***, is left on the soft wood. The mark may consist of an impression, scrape or gouge.

Tool marks should be photographed. The mark itself probably can't be individualized without recovering a tool, but careful examination may yield class characteristics indicating a high probability that a screwdriver, for example, was used. The technique a burglar uses to gain entry may help determine a modus operandi to research previous cases and help develop a suspect.

In-depth interviews should be conducted with the home or business owner. Have the premises been burglarized in the past? Is there anything unique about the burglary, such as time frame, a specific item stolen, or entry into a safe that would take special skills?

Crime Scene Evidence

In addition to fingerprints, the scene should be searched for other items of trace evidence, such as blood. An example is a burglar who cuts himself/herself crawling through a basement window. Also, search for hair, fibers, cigarettes, tools or anything else the burglar may have left behind.

In a burglary, the assistance of the victim may be required to identify what has been moved or touched and what does or does not belong. Because the burglar is often looking through things—desk or dresser drawers, for example—fingerprints are commonly found. Pawnshops and secondhand dealers should be contacted to determine whether property stolen in the burglary was sold to them.

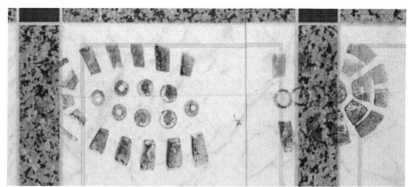

White gelatin lifters can be used to lift footprints or fingerprints left in blood.
Courtesy of BVDA International

A magnetic wand is used to apply powder that can be used to dust for fingerprints on wood, leather, plastic and other non-ferrous surfaces.
Photo Courtest of Tri-Tech, Inc.

Chapter Six Endnotes

1. Federal Bureau of Investigation, Crime in the United States-2003 (Washington DC: October 27, 2003, pp. 45-48).

2. U.S. Department of Justice, Federal Bureau of Investigation, Uniform Crime Reports 1975-2001 (Washington DC: U.S. Government Printing Office,1998).

Chapter Seven

Aggravated Assault, Motor Vehicle Theft and Arson

Aggravated Assault

The Uniform Crime Reporting program defines **aggravated assault** as the *unlawful attack by one person upon another for the purpose of inflicting severe or aggravated bodily injury*. Attempted aggravated assault involves the display of—or threat to use—a gun, knife, or other weapon. Attempted aggravated assault is included in this crime category because serious personal injury would likely result if the assault were completed.

An estimated 862,947 aggravated assaults were reported in 2005—25% of which involved a physical (hands, fists, feet, etc.) confrontation, and 21% of these assaults were committed with a firearm. About half (50%) of the aggravated assaults reported to the police are cleared by arrest.

There are differences between how individual states define aggravated assault as opposed to simple assault. The term "assault and battery" is rarely used today. Most of the difference between states and regions relative to defining what constitutes aggravated assault involve whether the assault or its attempt could or did result in serious physical injury to the person being assaulted and/or extreme indifference to human life. *Serious physical injury* is defined as *physical injury which creates a substantial risk of death, or which causes serious disfigurement or serious loss or impairment of the function of any bodily organ*. Thus, if Joe punches Sam in the mouth causing a laceration requiring three sutures, this would not rise to the level of "serious physical injury" but would be a simple assault.

Many states have created statutes separating the crime of assault into graduated degrees depending on the injury or likelihood of serious physical injury to the victim and use of threatened use of a weapon. Other factors may include whether the perpetrator was aided by one or more other persons; whether the victim is blind, disabled, pregnant or elderly; whether the victim was a corrections officer or the perpetrator was on parole; or the assault was committed with a motor vehicle. The statutes also outline the consequences—sentence and/or fines—resulting in being convicted of a specific degree of assault.

Assault in the First Degree, for example, is defined as causing physical injury to a person by means of a deadly weapon (a weapon designed specifically to kill—such as a gun—or a dangerous instrument, such as a baseball bat.

Assault in the Second Degree varies in the resulting threat to life in the consequence of the assault, and Assault in the Third Degree uses a term such as "physical injury" as opposed to "serious physical injury" to indicate the injury or threat of injury was not likely to cause death or serious disfigurement.

Investigating Assault Cases

There is little difference in the investigative process previously described in this book relative to homicide, as opposed to assault. The primary difference is that the victim lived. Obviously, the more serious the assault and likelihood of death, the more time and resources a department spends in investigating the crime. A simple fistfight with minor injuries would not require the same investigative resources as a person who was shot several times and who is in critical condition, but who eventually lives.

Patrol officers make the majority of assault arrests, not detectives. Patrol officers observe assaults while on patrol or respond to reports of assault in progress. This often results in an arrest with little need for subsequent investigation. If the assault rises to the level of a likelihood of death, then the same crime scene investigative processes described in other sections of this book apply.

Motor Vehicle Theft

According to the Federal Bureau of Investigation's Uniform Crime Report, there were approximately 1.2 million motor vehicles reported stolen in 2005. For UCR purposes, the term *motor vehicle* is defined as *self-propelled vehicles that run on the ground, but not on rails*. Among the motor vehicles included in this definition are automobiles, motorcycles, motor scooters, trucks, and buses. Not included are trains, farm and construction machinery, and boats. Theft of these types of vehicles is classified as a larceny under the Uniform Crime Reporting program. Although a large percentage of motor vehicles are later recovered, only about 13% of cases were reported to be cleared by arrest. Depending on which study is reviewed, the combined property value of motor vehicles stolen each year is now approaching $8 billion, averaging $6,173 per stolen vehicle.

Theft of a motor vehicle is a larceny. Although the statutory definition of what constitutes the crime of larceny under the category of motor vehicle theft varies from state to state, all include the basic elements of:

- *intent to permanently deprive the owner*
- *taking of another's property or,*
- *appropriating the property of another to oneself or a third person*

Unlike other larceny crimes, which may or may not be felonies, motor vehicle theft is a felony, although the classification of the type and severity of the felony often depends on the value of the vehicle stolen. Value is defined as the market value of the vehicle at the time and place of the crime. In Connecticut, the theft of a motor vehicle having a property value in excess of $10,000 is Larceny in the First Degree and a Class B Felony (punishable by not less than 1 year nor more than 20 years); if the value of the stolen vehicle is in excess of $5,000, it's a Larceny in the Second Degree and a Class C Felony (punishable by not less than 1 year nor more than 10 years. If the vehicle is valued less than $5,000, theft of it constitutes Larceny in the Third Degree and is a Class D Felony (punishable by not less than 1 year nor more than five years).

Because all states have a mandatory insurance requirement for motor vehicles and insurance companies require a police report before they will reimburse the owner, this crime is reported to law enforcement at a much higher rate than other crimes. Motor vehicles that are temporarily taken by persons having legal access to them—such as a spouse having joint custody over property—may not rise to the level of motor vehicle theft under the law, depending on the totality of circumstances of the individual case. Using a motor vehicle without the owner's permission also may be legally complicated if prior consent and/or lawful access had been granted.

In the majority of cases, persons arrested for the crime of motor vehicles theft are under the age of 25. Most motor vehicle thefts occur at night while the vehicle is parked at the victim's residence. Statistical indicators of low clearance rate, coupled with a high rate of motor vehicle theft, indicate the crime is difficult to solve.

Reasons Why Motor Vehicles are Stolen

Top reasons why motor vehicles are stolen:

1. The crime is easy to commit: Most stolen cars are unlocked, or keys are left in the ignition.

2. It is hard to trace stripped parts to stolen vehicles.

3. Many offenders (joy riders and those looking for temporary transportation) are quick to abandon the vehicle.

4. Car theft rings consist of organized, sophisticated professionals.

5. The sheer volume of caseload and the fact that motor vehicle thefts are crimes against property rather than persons diminish the resources the police usually can assign to these investigations.[1]

The typical categories of why cars are stolen are:

1. Joyriding
2. Stripping for parts
3. Criminal use
4. Resale
5. Insurance fraud

Joyriding

Most instances of **joyriding**—stealing a car on a dare or for the "thrill" of it—involve juveniles. If the keys are not in the vehicle, the ignition is "popped" by inserting a screwdriver or other metal object into the ignition column. Often the vehicle's radio and/or compact disk player is taken along with anything readily available in the vehicle. The car is usually quickly abandoned. Sometimes, a police officer will observe a motor vehicle being driven and occupied by several persons who appear too young to have an operator's license, coupled with other probable cause factors, and attempt to stop the car. This may result in a police chase (motor vehicle pursuit) of the vehicle which can be very dangerous depending on weather, road, location, speeds, and so on.

All police departments have policies and procedures relative to pursuing vehicles. These rules are grounded in the principle of whether catching and capturing the offender is more dangerous to the public than discontinuing active pursuit. For example, pursuing a stolen vehicle at high speed during peak rush hour traffic in a downtown area may be more dangerous to the community at large (accidents, injuries, death) than the actual crime—motor vehicle theft—represents to the general public. This doesn't mean the police stop looking for the vehicle and conducting a criminal investigation; it merely means a reasoned judgment is made based on the totality of circumstances as to whether a high-speed pursuit is prudent to continue if the only crime the occupants are being pursued for is motor vehicle theft and minor motor vehicle violations.

Stripping For Parts

Cars are stripped for profit. The term **stripping** refers to *stealing easily removed parts from a vehicle and selling them to individuals, salvage yards, flea markets, garages. and dealers.* Anything that can be removed quickly—such as tires, hub caps, radios, tape decks, wheels and batteries—are taken on the spot where the car is parked or the car is stolen and driven to a location—such as a private garage—where the perpetrator has more time to strip the car. This is different from a **chop-shop**, where thieves transport a stolen car to a garage and either receive cash on the spot or participate in completely dismantling the vehicle to sell the parts for profit.

A chop-shop removes and/or dismantles large components of the car, including the hood, doors, windows, fenders, air bags and just about everything except the engine and frame. The majority of these types of parts and vehicle components are not marked or stamped with identifying numbers, although there is a recent trend to place the VIN number (a seventeen letter and number combination vehicle identification number stamped on various parts of the car by the manufacturer) on parts of the car rather than just stamped/etched on the doorframe, engine block, and along the dashboard near the left front quarter panel.

The first symbol of the VIN number (which is a number) indicates the nation in which the vehicle was made. The second symbol, a letter, indicates who made the vehicle—the manufacturer—G standing for General Motors, for example. The third symbol, a number, indicates the make of the vehicle—F for Ford, C for Chevrolet, and so on. The next symbol indicates the type of restraints used in the vehicle (C for seatbelts). The next three symbols, all numbers, are the manufacturer's code for the position of the vehicle in the construction line and the body type of the vehicle. The next symbol, a letter, is the type of engine in the vehicle. The next symbol, a number, is a digit used to validate the entire VIN number. The tenth symbol, a letter, is the year the vehicle was made. The next symbol, a letter, indicates the city the auto manufacturing plant is located in, and the remaining six symbols, all numbers, are the production number of the vehicle.

Criminal Use

Criminals steal cars to be used as transportation in order to commit other crimes. All of us are familiar with the typical movie or television scenario of the getaway car in a bank robbery that was recently stolen in order to prevent it being directly linked to one or more of the participants. Stolen cars are also used in murders, kidnappings, and drive-by shootings. It's not unusual for such vehicles to be abandoned in a shopping mall, airport parking lot, or high-rise parking garage. The car is usually used to commit a crime within a short time before it's likely to be reported as stolen by its owner.

Speed of use is important to the criminal because of the ability of law enforcement enter VINs into a computer database, with instantaneous access and broadcast to officers on patrol. If the vehicle isn't going to be used right away, then the license plate is changed and/or the vehicle is quickly painted to alter its appearance. Sometimes the car is burned or hidden (merely covering the vehicle with a tarp buys time) or pushed into a body of water.

Car Theft Rings and Resale of Vehicles

Organized theft rings target specific cars to steal and sell them for resale to unscrupulous dealers, body shops and garages. Targeted vehicles are often sold out of state or shipped to order to other countries where orders have been placed for high-end luxury vehicles. The VIN numbers must be altered before it can be resold without being traced. After the VIN number is replaced and the car repainted, an application is made for a new certificate of title. Then a registration certificate and license plates are obtained. VIN numbers can be obtained from junked or salvaged vehicles of the same make or model and placed on the stolen vehicle after removing its VIN number.

Insurance Fraud

False insurance claims involving motor vehicles consist of a myriad of schemes ranging from stripping a vehicle, selling the parts, and then falsely reporting to the police the car was stolen to burning the vehicle and reporting it stolen. The losses to insurers for these type of fraudulent claims significantly affect everyone's individual insurance rates.

Investigating Motor Vehicle Theft

The sooner the investigator enters a stolen vehicle into the computerized data bank and broadcasts its description over the radio, the greater the chances the car will be recovered. In additional to local and state computer databases, stolen vehicles are entered in to the National Crime Information Center (NCIC).

Typical questions asked by an investigator conducting a preliminary investigation of a car being reported stolen include the following:

1. What is the make, model, license plate number, and VIN number of the vehicle?

2. Who is the registered owner(s) of the vehicle?

3. What are the names, ages, and addresses of all persons who have access to and/or operate the vehicle?

4. Where was the car parked when it was stolen?
    a. were the keys left in the vehicle?

5. What time was the vehicle parked in the location from which it was stolen?
    a. Who parked it in that location?
    b. Who discovered the vehicle missing?
    c. What time was the vehicle discovered to be missing?

6. Where was the driver of the car when the vehicle was stolen?

7. Was there anyone with the driver of the car when it was stolen?

---

8.   Who has keys to the vehicle? Where are the keys?

9.   Is the vehicle insured? Who is the insurer?

10. When was the vehicle last repaired? By what garage?

11. If financed, are the payments on the vehicle up to date?

12. Are there any other identifying features on or about the vehicle such as window and bumper stickers, dents, cracks in the windshield, etc.?

Once the vehicle's license plate number is broadcast, usually initially via radio, to patrol units, they will be on the lookout for the vehicle. Computerized technology in the police vehicle allows officers to quickly determine whether a vehicle is stolen. All patrol officers know the locations in their towns and cities where stolen vehicles are most likely to end up—high rise housing projects, mall parking lots, etc—and these are continuously checked and often the subject of police surveillance.

Experienced police officers also are keenly aware of erratic driver behavior, indicative that "crime may be afoot" and stop such vehicles to check the car and driver for appropriate documents. Such behavior may include a driver who suddenly changes direction and/or speed upon the approach of a police cruiser or who suddenly changes lanes, goes through stops signs and traffic lights, or engages in other reckless driving behavior.

Recovering Stolen Vehicles

Stolen cars are recovered in a variety of ways. Officers patrol a fixed area day after day and are alert to vehicles that have not moved for a long period of time, are improperly parked, seem out of place for the location (a new Jaguar parked in a low-income housing project) and so on. If the car still has a license plates, it is checked via computer by officers. Partially stripped vehicles and those without license plates require inspecting the interior and glove compartment, which commonly provides information as to the owner. If not, this information may be obtained from the vehicle's VIN number.

The frequency of motor vehicle thefts and recoveries and costs in terms of hours spent may preclude processing the vehicle for fingerprints and other associative evidence. However, if possible, or if the vehicles is known to be involved in criminal activity in addition to being stolen, the car should be thoroughly processed. In addition to dusting the car for prints, any container from which a biological sample—soda cups and straws, cigarette butts, blood and so on, should be preserved for DNA analysis. Damage indicating forced entry, tool impression marks, soil, hairs and fibers should be photographed and collected. They may link a suspect or victim to the vehicle and thus the crime.

In larger departments with specialized divisions, detectives are often assigned to follow up the initial patrol investigation into a reportedly stolen motor vehicle. Informants often pass along information on the more sophisticated organized car theft rings and on garages and chops shops that strip vehicles to resell parts or sell the car after altering the VIN number. This type of information, along with police surveillance and photography can result in obtaining a search and seizure warrant, and a police raid is conducted. In larger department's officers who have received specialized training in recognizing altered VIN numbers accompany the team raiding the location.

WAR STORY

When I was a detective, my partner and I were summoned to a large, multi-level parking garage where hundreds of cars were parked every day. A patrol officer had made a habit of driving through the garage on a daily basis and noticed one particular vehicle had been parked in the garage for an extended period of time. The vehicle had been backed up against the cement wall of the garage and was missing the front license plate. The doors to the car were locked, but the officer noticed what appeared to be dried blood on the top of the trunk of the car. This type of vehicle didn't have the VIN number displayed along the inner windshield.

We didn't want to tow the vehicle for fear of destroying any evidence, and although we were able to enter the front door with a slim-jim, the steering column was locked and we couldn't get the car in gear to move it forward so we could pop the trunk with a crowbar. The glove compartment was empty, but there were several rags on the back seat with what appeared to be blood and semen stains on them.

We ended up calling in the Evidentiary Services Unit to process the outside of the car and obtaining a search and seizure warrant to search it.

In the trunk of the car we found a 25-year-old woman who had been bound, gagged, and strangled. The vehicle had been reported stolen a week prior to its appearance in the parking garage.

This is a good example of the type of case involving a vehicle being stolen and then used in the commission of a crime.

Arson

The Uniform Crime Reporting Program defines **arson** as *any willful malicious burning or attempt to burn, with or without intent to defraud, a dwelling house, public building, motor vehicle or aircraft, or person property of another.* Only fires that investigators find to fall within the above definition are classified as an arson in the UCR, not fires of suspicious or of unknown origin. There were 67,504 arson offenses reported to the UCR program in 2005, with an average loss, per arson offense, of $14,910. Arsons involving structures (residential, storage, public, etc.) accounted for 43.6% of the total number of arson offenses. Arson of industrial and manufacturing structures resulted in the highest average dollar losses—approximately $356,324 per arson.

In most areas of the country, arson investigation falls under the purview of state and local fire marshals. In other areas, the police have jurisdiction along with fire authorities. Specialized knowledge, skill and equipment is required to conduct an arson investigation, and the majority of police departments do not have trained arson investigators. Investigating arsons is further complicated by the fact that most evidence is rendered unusable due to the destructive nature of the fire and efforts by firefighters to put the fire out.

Investigating Suspected Arson

Because of the technical nature of fire investigation, it is not the intention of this book to provide a detailed analysis of how to investigate arson cases. However, some key points are of special interest to police investigators, especially if a person died as a result of the fire.

Every fire should be viewed as a potential crime scene. Once the fire is extinguished, entry should be made as soon as possible. A thorough search of the premises for survivors and/or bodies is followed by crime scene photography and video recording. Based on their experience and training, firefighters are the best source to recognize whether a fire is unusual and arson is suspected.

Investigators search for incendiary evidence, which includes the burning characteristics of the fire, fire scene debris, and use of accelerants. Gasoline is the most common accelerant used to commit the crime of arson. Most accelerants have detectable odors and smoke coloring. The primary focus of every arson investigation is the fire's point of origin.

If arson is suspected, investigators concentrate on motive as a primary solvability factor. Motives for committing arson may include profit, crime concealment, vandalism, revenge, pyromania, etc. Thus, the teaming of fire and police investigators—each having different skills sets—is very beneficial in investigating crimes of arson.

Case Law

When can the police and/or fire investigators enter a building after a fire has been extinguished to obtain evidence as to how the fire started? In a 1978 Supreme Court decision (*Michigan v. Tyler*), the court ruled that "immediate investigation" may be necessary to preserve evidence and investigators can remain in the building for a "reasonable time" to investigate the cause of the blaze without a search and seizure warrant. However, subsequent visits to gather evidence from the scene do require a search warrant.

Chapter Seven Endnotes

Criminal Investigation, A method for reconstructing the past, James W. Ostenburg & Richard W. Ward, Anderson Publishing, 2004

ADVANCING TO AN INVESTIGATIVE POSITION

Chapter Eight

The Testing Process

Introduction

This section of the book is designed to help you prepare for advancement to an investigative position. You'll be involved in a very competitive process designed to predict which candidates will be most successful in performing the job. Unlike in the private sector, opportunities for promotion in policing may occur only four or five times in a twenty-five-year career. Often, only a tenth of a point separates those who get promoted from those who end up near the top of an expired civil service list. Persistence, motivation, and consistent studying are the keys to success. It's going to take lots of hard work, dedication, and commitment for you to succeed.

This part of the book is designed to give you a competitive edge in your promotional examinations, prepare you for excellence and motivate you to succeed. Regardless of whether you'll be taking a written examination or oral test, this book will sharpen your test-taking skills and provide a base of knowledge designed to position you for excellence.

Because you're already a police officer and have passed a host of different types of tests to get the job and graduate from the police academy, you're probably pretty good at studying on your own and have used a variety of techniques to prepare for examinations. The type of learning with which you're most comfortable may be with a teacher with whom you can have personal contact. You have used your sense of sight, listened and asked questions. There was a give-and-take between you, the instructor, and the other members of the class. Your teacher told you what to do, and could even physically show you how to do it. You learned through repetition.

When studying alone, you outlined the chapter, highlighted or transferred what you considered to be important information onto index cards so you could memorize what you thought was going to be on the test. This is the method most of us in policing use to study for different types of examinations.

This part of the book proposes a different approach to the learning process. It outlines a guide and gives you a how-to-do-it methodology. We are limited by a one-way communication process: I write, you read. Most authors communicate with readers material that has already been written before by merely using different words. We're going to use a different approach to learning: the process of *discovery*.

Discovery is finding out through exploration, reading, observing, discerning, and original thinking. Your prior learning (professional, educational and life experiences) serve as a foundation or platform onto which new learning can be grafted and linked together. Discovery is similar to a martial arts philosophy symbolizing a series of life-long challenges, each of which is at a slightly higher plateau. Experience, intuition and deductive reasoning are combined through a step-by-step process that will push, pull and inspire you toward excellence.

Remember the old adage, "You can lead a horse to water, but you can't make it drink"? While this may be true, you *can* make a horse thirsty. My job as your coach and guide is to do just that.

Reading for Understanding

The first step in the discovery process is to make certain you know how to read for understanding, insight, and retention, not just to obtain information. Although I hope you find this section of the book interesting, it's not designed to be read as you would a newspaper or novel.

Depending on the variables presented in the initial contact, police administrators should insure that personnel are trained to do the following:

- Discover the knowledge, skills and abilities you'll be tested for.

- Understand how to excel on the various types of tests.

- Take practice tests and track your progress.

- Gain greater understanding of investigative theories and concepts.

You need to read this entire the book twice, using a different technique each time. The first time is easy: Simply read without trying to learn anything in particular. Merely acquaint yourself with the contents of the book to get an overview of what's offered. Don't worry about any of the practice examinations at this stage. In fact, skip over them entirely.

After reading the book through the first time, put it aside and gather the following items:

1. A dictionary. Not a little hand-held copy, but a big, thick edition.

2. A large notebook: the kind that divides into several sections.

3. Two or three highlighters and some thick rubber bands.

4. About three hundred 3"x5" white index cards.

5. A tape recorder and some blank tapes.

6. A copy of the test announcement for the examinations you'll be taking.

7. Any books or other materials that the test announcement states will be used as reference guides for the examination.

8. A copy of your department's procedural manual, rules and regulations, and/or general orders.

9. A copy of your state's Law Enforcement Officer Field Manual, which typically has sections describing criminal statutes and applicable investigative case law in areas such as search and seizure, probable cause, arrest, interrogation, etc.

Motivation

Continuously motivating and disciplining yourself to prepare for your exam is an important factor that will separate you from your competition. If you don't prepare adequately, someone else will get promote instead of you. It has been my experience that what prevents most police officers from being promoted to detective is that they simply don't study hard enough for the tests. Promotion is not a matter of who is the best cop or even who would make the best detective; it's a question of who scores the highest on test day.

So how do you motivate yourself?

First, are you serious about putting in the time and effort you know it's going to take to come out number one on the list? You're a busy person, and other people are constantly pulling you in different directions. You're going to face countless hours of studying without really knowing what will be on the tests. You'll have to take time away from your family and friends. You will be prone to rationalization, thinking that politics and other interdepartmental jousting for position will prevent you from being a detective anyway, so why bother going through the process? You know that getting promoted will mean more responsibility, longer hours, and perhaps even less pay when you figure in the overtime that can be made in patrol. You may be thinking that the testing system is unfair, biased against you and bears no relationship to the street.

This type of negative thinking is just what your competition is hoping for. Recognize the fact that you have your future, and the future of your family in your hands right now. You can come out number one in the testing process, and, if you're sharp enough, you will get promoted. Negative thinking, rationalization and procrastination are not the traits of a person motivated to spend long hours studying, so promise yourself to do everything in your power to succeed. If you don't develop techniques to increase your ability to stay focused on getting promoted, chances are you won't achieve your goal. The competition is too great. Stay focused. Every morning from now until test day, ask yourself what you have done to excel in the promotional process.

Energizing the Learning Process

Now that you've gathered the things you'll need, it's time to read the book a second time. This time, it will be harder. Because reading comprehension is such a critical component in the types of tests you'll be taking, let's begin by improving your ability in that area right now.

First of all, find a quiet place to study. Remove or resist distractions such as television, radio, video games, e-mail and the Internet. Then, read this book very slowly from the beginning, disciplining yourself to pay strict attention to every single word. While you're reading, don't allow your mind to wander. Your ability to understand what you read is an important skill in test taking.

Written communication consists of two types of words: ordinary words and important words. Tests are no different. The ordinary words are the prepositions, conjunctions, articles, adverbs and most of the adjectives and verbs forming the skeleton on which the key concepts (the important words) hang. The very fact that you don't immediately understand a word, or a series of words, in a sentence should alert you to the need to take the time to look up the word in the dictionary and analyze its meaning.

Most of us have developed the bad habit of skipping over words we're not familiar with, figuring we'll understand what the writer means by the context. This works rather well in reading newspapers, magazines and fiction, but it's really only scanning, not reading for understanding. Writers of instructional textbooks and test analysts write in a style that gives clues to what they think is important by using bold type, italics, quotation marks, underlining, or by discussing a term's definition. Pay attention to periods, exclamation points, and commas as well.

So get out your dictionary, notebook, pencil or pen and highlighter. As you're slowly reading the material, sentence by sentence, develop the habit of highlighting key words and concepts. Every single time you come across a word in a sentence that you don't immediately know the meaning of, look it up in the dictionary, cross the word out, and write the definition above it or in the margin. Write the heading **Key Words and Concepts** in your notebook, and list each of the words and its meaning in that section. Return and re-read the sentence with the definition of the important word (it's important to you if you don't understand its meaning) in mind. Our understanding of words directly affect how we communicate.

Emphasis can change the meaning of a word or an entire sentence. For example, here is essentially the same sentence with different emphasis on key words.

Read the following out loud:

The detective asked the suspect whether he saw the woman steal the money. The suspect replied, "I didn't see the woman steal the money."

Pretty clear, right? But what if I were to write it this way?

The detective asked the suspect whether he saw the woman steal the money.

The suspect looked surprised, pointed to himself, and shook his head. He said, "*I* didn't see the woman steal the money!"

Notice how a brief description of the suspect's body language adds to your understanding. The word "I" in **bold italics** suggests emphasis, and there's an exclamation point at the end. The inference is that the *suspect* didn't see the woman steal the money, but someone else did see it.

What if I were to write it this way?

"I didn't see the **woman** steal the money!"

Because the word "woman" has been emphasized and is followed by an exclamation point, the meaning of the sentence is that the suspect saw *someone* steal the money, but it wasn't necessarily the woman.

Although this may seem pretty basic, it's not. Many police examinations at the detective level contain sections that require you to either read a short essay and then answer four or five multiple-choice questions or construct an essay citing what your response would be to a hypothetical question.

I want you to sharpen your ability to read with understanding in order to avoid choosing the wrong answer simply because you didn't grasp the subtle changes that little things like punctuation and key words can mean in the essay. If you're required to write a short essay as part of your examination, clear, concise answers are best.

This could be a typical essay question:

> Describe your experience in searching for, identifying, and securing evidence at a crime scene, especially as it relates to what evidentiary and investigative value firearms, blood, semen, hairs, fibers, tool marks, fingerprints and impressions have to the investigative process.

In order to write an acceptable response to this essay question, you must be familiar with basic investigative and forensic concepts. Take out a pad of paper and try answering the question right now. After you're finished, review the essay from the position of a test analyst grading your response. Upon completing this exercise, review the investigative study guide CD. Is your answer complete? Could you have written a more thorough response?

Before the Test Announcement

Many of us make the mistake of waiting for an official test announcement before beginning to study, and actively position ourselves for advancement within the organization. You should always be preparing for the examination to the next level, and you can't afford to wait if you want to be competitive. If your agency's rumor mill is pounding the drums about a promotional test for detective, it's probably true. Retirement is the primary indicator for an upcoming vacancy in the detective ranks. In organizations that have labor/management contracts, this historically has a bearing on when people choose to retire due to pre-scheduled contractual raises and other benefits for which they may have been waiting.

Check your department's seniority list to see how many other people have the necessary tenure and other qualifications to be eligible to take the examination you're testing for. Know who your competitors are and how they have positioned themselves within the organization. Because many departments adhere to the "Rule of Three" (the chief can select from any of the top three candidates on the final eligible list), this may be a good time to form organizational alliances with those who can further your career.

Consider the following:

What can you do to foster the belief in the chief's mind that your promotion will add strength to the investigative team, fulfill organizational goals and contribute to mission accomplishment?

Do you have a clear understanding of what the chief wants?

Are you a team player? Do you consistently put organizational goals ahead of your own personal goals?

In his 1971 book, *Executive Career Strategy*, author Alan N. Schoonmaker makes the following suggestions:

1. Do excellent work.

2. Become visible within the organization.

3. Present the right image.

4. Avoid becoming deadwood.

5. Control resources, especially information.

6. Develop good personal relationships.[1]

What's on the Test?

There are other significant things you can do before the promotional examination announcement is officially posted. Find out who took the last promotional examinations for detective and came out number one or two. People who have been promoted are often eager to talk about how they aced the test. Usually, they're willing to answer any of your questions, and there's nothing ethically wrong with picking the brains of people who have already succeeded. Your competition will be doing the same thing.

Ask high scorers the following questions:

1. *What type of examination did you take? Was it a written test, consisting of multiple-choice questions? Did it contain any true/false or essay questions? Was it given at an assessment center, and if so, which types of scenarios were used?*

2. *What were the major subject areas covered? How investigative-oriented was it? Did the test ask questions about crime scenes, forensics, DNA, case law, state statutes, search warrants, etc.?*

3. *What type of marking system was used to correct the written examination? Did wrong answers count against you, or were only correct answers totaled? Were those who scored less than 70% allowed to take the oral examination, or were they eliminated from the process?*

4. *How long did you have to wait to receive your score? Was it immediately corrected by computer, or was there an extended wait?*

5. *What type of oral examination was given? One oral with three panelists, or a series of different orals scheduled throughout the day or over a series of days? Was it a "technical" oral or a "traditional" oral?*

6. *Which books were listed on the examination reference posting? Do you still have them? If so, may I borrow them? From which books were most of the questions taken?*

7. *Did the test cover department orders and procedures, rules and regulations, state statues, or department manuals?*

8. *Did the test consist of an evaluation of training and experience? If so, what type of training and experience counted the highest: college education, graduation from investigative schools and seminars, investigative-type assignments, length of service?*

Your promotional examination will be created either by someone in your municipality's personnel department in coordination with the chief, a test consultant, or a professional test preparation service. The test questions for investigative promotional examinations are taken from books on criminal investigation, department orders, rules and regulations, procedural manuals, training bulletins and state statutes. Because the investigative concepts and other material relative to policing changes infrequently (with the exception of forensics and technology), it's likely that the material used on the last test will also be on yours. Promotional examinations are extremely costly to create and administer. Given the reality of shrinking city, town, and state budgets, it's not often cost-effective to create a new test.

Undoubtedly, there will have been new court decisions and forensic developments since the last time a test was given. However, concepts evolve slowly in our profession. For example, major topic areas, such as "Interview and Interrogation" or "Search and Seizure," have changed very little over the past several years. So, it's worth the investment to obtain materials pertinent to these subject areas and begin studying before the official examination announcement.

In larger departments, you may find promotional reference material in the police academy library. In smaller organizations, check with the department's training officer to see whether you can get a copy of the last promotional test announcement. The books and materials used as references for that exam will be listed. You can buy or order the books at your local bookstore and find the other study materials in department binders or manuals. You can also often find the books you need at bargain prices online form sites such as Half.com, Amazon.com or eBay. Just be sure to order the most up-to-date editions so that you don't wind up studying from outdated books.

The following reference sources have often been used in the past by test analysts in creating police promotional examinations and are valuable additions to any investigator's library:

— *Criminal Investigation, 2ⁿᵈ Edition* by Ronald F. Becker, 2004, Jones and Bartlett Publishers Inc., ISBN 0763731684

— *Criminal Investigation, 8ᵗʰ Edition* by Wayne W. Bennett and Kären M. Hess, 2006, Wadsworth Publishing, ISBN 0495093408

— *Criminal Investigation, 9ᵗʰ Edition* by Charles R Swanson, Neil C. Chamelin, Leonard Territo and Robert W. Taylor, 2005, McGraw-Hill, ISBN 0073212784

— *Criminal Investigation: A Method for Reconstructing the Past, 5ᵗʰ Edition* by James W. Osterburg and Richard H. Ward, 2007, Anderson Publishing, ISBN 1593454295

— *Criminalistics: An Introduction to Forensic Science, 9ᵗʰ Edition* by Richard Saferstein, 2006, Prentice Hall, ISBN 0132216558

A head start in the studying process will result in large dividends on test day. It's been my experience that high promotional test scores have a direct correlation with the amount of effort expended in preparing and studying.

Types of Test Questions

There are two types of test questions commonly used in written and oral police examinations: generic and procedural. ***Generic questions*** are not specific to the duties performed by a detective in your department. They are broad in scope and generally deal with what all investigators should do in any police department. ***Procedural questions*** are specific to what a detective would be required to do based on department orders, guidelines, procedures, and rules and regulations. For example, if an exam question dealt with securing a firearm found at a crime scene, there are general things all police detectives should do, whether in Dallas, New York City, or Philadelphia, and then there are the specific responsibilities in your department. The former are generic, and the latter, procedural.

It's critical to determine whether your promotional examination will have generic questions, procedural questions, or a combination of both. Many cities use "canned" tests that are developed by companies specializing in creating promotional examinations. If your test wasn't created by your municipality, the "canned" exam will consist of only generic questions. Written tests often come down to choosing the most correct answer between two very similar alternatives. Knowing whether your answer selection should be based on the requirements of your department, as opposed to a generic response, can help add points to your final score.

The Test Announcement

The city or town is required by its charter, and/or personnel regulations and labor laws, to notify those eligible to fill vacancies in positions of a higher classification. This notification must include the method by which a selection for promotion will be made. Most cities fulfill this obligation by creating a ***test announcement*** that is posted in a prominent place within the department and/or mailed to eligible candidates. The test announcement contains a wealth of information important to you in planning your study program. If it's not individually distributed, make a copy for yourself. A description of the critical sections with an explanation of how you can use them to plan your program of study follows.

Eligibility Criteria

Most police departments in the United States fall under the civil service testing system, which was created to protect police selection and promotion processes from political interference. Police promotional examinations have been so heavily litigated that personnel departments now go great lengths to ensure promotional examinations, and the process under which they are created will withstand review by the courts. At the same time, the minimum requirements for promotion are becoming more stringent. Many departments require a combination of job tenure and advanced education. Invariably, the minimum standard will include a length-of-service requirement, which varies from city to city.

However, if the time-in-grade requirement to be eligible to take the test is three years, for example, and you fall several months short, immediately begin petitioning your personnel department to be allowed to take the test using the following rationale: Your tenure may qualify you for eligibility at the time the test is given. The cut-off date for application to take the test may be in June, for example, but the written test won't be given until August. Would you have enough tenure by the time the testing process is completed to meet the seniority requirement? You have nothing to lose and everything to gain by asking questions. Union officials can apply pressure to revise the length-of-service restriction because of the effect it will have on a large segment of its members.

Duties and Responsibilities

The test announcement will outline the duties and responsibilities those giving the examination have determined are necessary to successfully perform the job. Using one of your highlighters, mark the major topic areas. You'll see general headings such as "Conducts Follow-Up Investigations," "Responds to Major Crime Scenes" and "Prepares Evidence for Court and Other Official Proceedings." Write each of these major headings across the top of an index card for future reference. You'll have to use several to complete this process.

Knowledge, Skills and Abilities (KSA)

This section of the test announcement is of particular importance because, in many ways, it tells you what's going to be on the test. In order for the examination to be valid (and therefore defensible in court), it must be job related. The purpose of the examination process is to impartially and objectively evaluate the knowledge, skills and aptitude of each candidate so that the candidates can be ranked in the order of their relative competence. Another purpose of the exam is to reject candidates who lack sufficient competence to perform the duties of the position.

This part of the test announcement outlines the basic knowledge a detective should have and be able to demonstrate: in other words, the necessary skills and abilities. Many personnel analysts confuse the terms *skills* and *abilities*. An *ability* is an individual trait you possess. You're either born with it or develop it as you mature. A *skill* defines whether you are able to do something (perform a specific job task, for example) after you have received appropriate training.

The reason this distinction is so important is that many police detective tests evaluate candidates for skills that wouldn't be present until after the person is in the position and receives training on how to do it.

The KSA area on the test announcement might be quite specific and might give further insight into what the test will cover. Highlight these topics and place them on your index cards next to the appropriate "Example of Duties" section.

Methods of Selection

This is the most important section of the test announcement. It explains the type and various parts of the examination, the skill level and depth of understanding required, the relative weights of each type or part of the test, and the minimum passing score, if there is one. It also explains how the test will be graded.

Methods of selecting candidates for promotion vary from one municipality to another. Here is an example of how this section might look:

Parts	Weight	Passing Score
Written Examination	45%	70%
Oral Examination	40%	70%
Time in Service	5%	—
Performance Evaluation	5%	—
Education	5% Bachelor Degree*	—

*Bachelor Degree: 3 additional points for graduate degree

In some departments, the oral examination counts for up to 50% of the final grade. Others add points for veteran's preference, residency, education, seniority, performance evaluations, or for being a member of a "protected class." This section informs applicants of the suggested reference material from which the test is constructed.

There's also usually a caveat that states, "Listed will be books, manuals, department procedures, rules and regulations," etc. Obtain all of these materials as quickly as possible and begin studying.

Qualification procedures for different phases of the examination are also explained. A minimum passing grade on the written test is often required in order to be eligible to take the oral examination. Any physical examination requirements will be explained along with the date of expiration of the promotion list.

The date and location of the first phase of the test will also be given. Usually, there is a statement that further information on the test specifics will be mailed to candidates.

There are sections of this book devoted specifically to preparing you for the various types of examinations, but the above factors may influence your program of study.

Submitting Applications

This section of the test announcement explains where applications may be obtained and the deadline for their submission. The application will be reviewed at many different levels and may eventually end up at your oral board.

Do not hand-write your application unless the directions specifically require you to do so. Instead, you should type it. Be certain that all of the blocks are filled in completely. Make a copy for yourself.

If possible, deliver the application in person. Obtain the name of the person that you give it to, and request that it be dated and time-stamped in your presence. In some departments, ties on the exam are broken based on the time and date the application was submitted—a fact usually not mentioned on the test announcement or by the person to whom you hand your application.

In other departments, seniority in job classification breaks ties. Your standing on the department's seniority list is often determined by the date of appointment to your current rank and further classified by your final rank-ordered standing in the police academy.

If either of these methods is used to break ties on your promotional tests, you can verify it in your state, city or town personnel rules. Familiarize yourself with the process, and photocopy relevant sections.

Sample Test Announcement

The following is an example of a recent test announcement for the position of Police Detective:

THE CITY OF ANYWHERE
WRITTEN EXAMINATION: POLICE DETECTIVE

Areas to be tested and examples of question topics:

LAWS AND LEGAL GUIDELINES RELATING TO POLICE WORK

Examples: The State General Statutes and applicable federal and state court decisions (including Supreme Court decisions); laws of arrest, search and seizure; probable cause; laws and legal guidelines relative to interviews and interrogations; police ethics; affidavits, arrest, and search and seizure warrants; use of force; City of Anywhere Police department policy and procedure relating to the above.

CONDUCTING PRELIMINARY INVESTIGATIONS

Examples: Knowledge of how to prepare investigative notes, records, and reports in a timely and accurate fashion to record a crime scene; rules of evidence, including chain of custody; crime scene procedures; identifying, gathering and preserving evidence; knowledge and ability relative to taking statements and confessions; use of informants; narcotics and dangerous drug investigations; knowledge of and ability to apply legal guidelines to mug shots, photographs and line-up procedures; City of Anywhere Police department policy and procedure relating to the above.

CONDUCTING ON-GOING CRIMINAL INVESTIGATIONS

Examples: Establishing priorities, problem-solving and decision-making; gathering information from people and records; court testimony and preparing a case for court presentation; knowledge and ability in applying General State Statutes and Supreme Court guidelines and decisions to criminal investigations; knowledge relative to the various rules of evidence; characteristics and modus associated with common crimes, such as robbery, burglary, auto theft and narcotics and associated investigative techniques in preventing and solving; City of Anywhere Police department policy and procedure relating to the above.

PARTS AND WEIGHTS

The examination process will consist of a written and an oral examination. A score of less than 70% on the written examination will eliminate a candidate from going forward in the testing process.

Written Examination	40% of the Total Test Score
Oral Examination	50% of the Total Test Score
Performance Evaluation	10% of the Total Score

Note: Other areas may be tested. See reading list below.

READING LIST

1. *Criminal Investigation: A Method for Reconstructing the Past, 5th Edition* by James W. Osterburg and Richard H. Ward. 2007, Anderson Publishing Company, Cincinnati, Ohio.
2. State of Anywhere Law Enforcement Officers' Field Manual, current issue.
3. The City of Anywhere Police Policies and Procedures

Chapter Seven Endnotes

1. Alan N. Schoonmaker, *Executive Career Strategy*, American Management Association,1971

Chapter Nine

The Written Examination

The methodology used by your department to test candidates for promotion may be explained in one or more of the following:

1. The city, state or town charter.

2. The city, state or town personnel rules.

3. Labor/management contract.

4. Labor board decisions.

5. Court decisions.

Most police organizations follow strict procedures for administering promotional examinations. Typical test announcements outline the who, what, where, when and how of the test administration. Obtain a copy of everything relating to testing, promotion, filling vacancies, appeals, eligibility lists, etc. Highlight all pertinent information and place it in a folder marked "Promotional File" along with a copy of your application. If your test score ends up being tied with another officer's, or if the mandated process hasn't been followed, you may need this research material in order to file an appeal.

Appealing Written Tests

Police promotional examinations have become heavily litigated during the past several years. Promotional examinations are only as good as the people who create and administer them, and you have every right to question any part of the testing process. Ordinarily, the personnel rules of the municipality outline a formal process for appealing or protesting test questions, parts of the examination, etc.

For example, after the written test is administered, many departments provide candidates with a tentative answer key to the test and forms with which to appeal specific questions. So, if the answer key indicates that the correct answer is (B), and you answered (C) because that's what the study material referenced in the test announcement indicated was the correct answer, you certainly have the right to point this out. If you cite the reference from which you derived your answer, you may receive credit for the question. If you disagree with the test administrator's decision, you can take the matter to court, but this is often very time consuming and costly. If the examination is for a management position within the department, you're probably outside of an employee union and would have to personally bear the cost for any civil litigation involved. It's important to keep carefully documented records on the entire testing process in case the test isn't administered properly.

Constructing Written Tests

One of the reasons so many people fail written examinations at the investigative level is that they study the wrong material or use the wrong study techniques. Don't make the mistake of studying for your promotional examinations the same way you studied for exams in college or at training seminars. Those tests usually required you to recall specific facts from a relatively narrow band of subject matter.

Promotional examinations cover much broader topic areas, and to be successful in taking them, you must be knowledgeable about basic principles and concepts rather than specific areas. Memorizing definitions and steps associated with various investigative processes won't get you where you need to be.

It's important to memorize some material, but if the information you memorized doesn't appear as one of the questions on the test, it will be of little help to you. Focus your studying on understanding basic principles and concepts. Using this technique will ensure that regardless of whether the questions concern forensics, investigative techniques or the principle of investigation, you'll have a better chance of choosing the correct answer.

Test Validity and Reliability

Why is it that the process used to test police and other civil service candidates for promotion often ends up being litigated in the courts, resulting in costly and extended delays in promoting candidates? Why have an increasing number of police officers lost confidence in the types of examinations used to test who among them has demonstrated that they are the most capable of performing the job successfully? The answer to these questions is that many of the testing methods used by police departments bear little relationship to actually doing the job, and the candidates know it.

Police promotional examinations that consistently withstand review by the courts and successfully match candidates with job performance have two things in common: test validity and reliability. A 1968 Supreme Court decision, *Griggs v. Duke Power*, requires that promotional examinations have a direct relationship to success on the job and that a "test which fails a higher percentage of minority applicants is discriminatory." Research into promotional testing by the nationally recognized Police Foundation indicated that "What is prohibited is the use of tests and other selection techniques which tend to disproportionately reject members of various classes heretofore discriminated against (e.g., minorities, women, Vietnam Era Veterans, etc.) and which cannot or have not been demonstrated by the employer to measure and reflect occupational requirement."

In another important court decision, *Brito v. Zia*, the Tenth Circuit Court ruled that a "performance evaluation is also a test and must be validated according to the Equal Opportunity Employment Act of 1972 relative to employment testing."

For a test to be valid, the questions, when taken in their totality, must specifically relate to job performance. In an exam for detective, for example, it would be improper to ask a test question involving the specific duties performed by a police sergeant. The stronger the relationship between test results and job performance, the more effective the test is as a selection tool. When scores and job performance are unrelated, the test is invalid and should not be used for selection. For a promotional test to be reliable, it must consistently and dependably measure those characteristics needed to perform a job properly over a period of time.

There are several ways that those who create promotional examinations can ensure that the tests are related to job performance (that they measure what they're supposed to be measuring). One method is for the test to perform a job task analysis—a systematic process that defines the exact tasks, knowledge, abilities and performance behaviors requisite for performing a job successfully over a period of time. In conducting a job task analysis, the test analyst writes down in logical sequence the steps that must be taken by the person completing a job in order to perform it properly.

The person creating the test must be careful to differentiate between the characteristics an individual must possess before assuming the position of, for example, police detective, and those normally obtained through experience and training after promotion. One of the problems often cited in police testing is the tendency to promote people before determining whether they have the characteristics necessary to perform the job—one of the primary disadvantages of using, for example, seniority as a criterion for promotion. Tenure doesn't necessarily mean that a candidate possesses the traits necessary to become a good police investigator.

What is it that those now performing the job for which you are testing "do" and "how" do they do it? What steps are required? What unique characteristics are important? What job tasks do detectives spend most of their time performing? The complexities of the job often demand that those in investigative positions have a wide body of knowledge and experience to draw on in order to be successful. As a career police professional, recognize that promotions must be sought after and won. The successful candidate for promotion is aggressive and accepts responsibility for his or her own career management.

Test developers ensure that exams are job-related through observation (actually observing a representative sample of the people in the position performing job tasks), by completing behavior and job task checklists and surveys, and by conducting face-to-face interviews.

In conducting interviews, the test analyst meets with individuals who hold the rank/position for which the test is being designed and asks them predetermined questions in order to find out how frequently they perform a specific job function and what degree of importance they attach to it. The following is a sample of what a test expert might find are some of the knowledge, skills and personal traits needed for the position of police detective.

This partial list is for illustrative purposes and is in no particular order relative to most versus least important.

Detective Job Task Analysis

KNOWLEDGE, SKILLS, ABILITIES, AND PERSONAL TRAITS

1. Knowledge of how and ability to prepare statements, affidavits, arrest, and search and seizure warrants.

2. Knowledge and ability in applying sound police practices and City of Anywhere Police procedures to crime scenes, and evidence collection and preservation.

3. Knowledge and ability relative to the taking of statements and confessions.

4. Knowledge of what constitutes a lawful arrest.

5. Skill in organizing ideas and written materials in a logical, coherent manner.

6. Knowledge and ability to apply Supreme Court decisions to police situations.

7. Knowledge and ability in applying probable cause in police situations.

8. Knowledge and ability to apply legal guidelines to mug shots, photographs, and line-up procedures

9. Knowledge of how to use criminal and other records in an investigation.

10. Knowledge and ability relative to custody and chain of evidence.

11. Knowledge and ability to conduct a crime scene search for evidence.

12. Knowledge of how to properly identify, develop, interpret and preserve physical evidence.

13. Ability to make and write reports of cases, complaints and investigations.

14. Ability to properly prepare investigative notes.

15. Knowledge and ability to apply state statutes and Anywhere Police guidelines relative to the use of force.

16. Knowledge of how to cultivate and use informants and the Anywhere Police policy relative to informants.

17. Knowledge relative to conducting investigations involving narcotics and dangerous drugs.

18. Knowledge and ability relative to testifying in court.

19. Knowledge and ability relative to the various rules of evidence.

20. Skill in maintaining a cooperative relationship with other agencies and public and private officials.

21. Knowledge of how and ability in applying sound police practices and Anywhere Police procedures to crime scenes, evidence collection, and preservation.

22. Knowledge of how to reconstruct the method in which a crime occurred.

23. Knowledge of how to prepare investigative notes, records, reports, and photographs in an accurate manner to record a crime scene.

24. Knowledge of the methods of establishing the cause, manner and time of death.

25. Knowledge relative to conducting investigations into street gangs and criminal enterprises.

26. Knowledge and ability relative to testifying in court.

27. Knowledge of laws relative to wiretapping, bugs, pen registers, monitoring conversations and visual enhancement devices.

28. Understanding of how to conduct a one-on-one confrontation.

29. Understanding of how to conduct a surveillance and the legal issues involved.

30. Knowledge relative to conducting arson investigations.

31. Knowledge relative to conducting missing persons investigations.

32. Knowledge relative to conducting undercover investigations.

33. Knowledge relative to conducting sex crimes investigations.

34. Knowledge, skill, and ability in questioning complainants, witnesses, victims and suspects.

35. Knowledge of how to recognize, collect and analyze modus operandi records and activities.

36. Ability to deal with others in a tactful, sensitive, impartial manner.

37. Ability to speak clearly and precisely.

38. Ability to choose appropriate language to fit the situation when speaking to a group or individual.

39. Skill in organizing ideas, concepts and materials in a logical, coherent fashion for oral or written presentations.

40. Ability to determine how to get the job done with resources available.

41. Ability to group and schedule activities.

42. Ability to use computer systems in police-related problem solving.

43. Ability to put department goals ahead of personal goals.

It's quite a list, isn't it? However, if you correlate a job-task analysis, observe people currently in the position who are successful, and review your department's orders outlining the duties and responsibilities of the position you will be tested for, you will gain a fairly accurate picture of what's going to be covered in your promotional examination. All departments include the job description for the various positions within the organization in their orders and procedures—a document that's one of the basic tools used in the creation of promotional examinations.

Your test will compare performance (on a multiple-choice test in which you select the answer, for example) with predetermined criteria as described above. The kind of promotional examinations used most often are criterion-type tests that measure your response against a predetermined, presumably correct standard.

Multiple-choice questions are used most often in promotional examinations because they have the following advantages:

1. They lend themselves to more reliable answers through standardized test items.

2. In contrast to true/false questions, in multiple-choice examinations, the effect of guessing is reduced.

3. Answers that are almost correct can be added to require a discriminating choice between two close answers, only one of which is correct.

4. They can be quickly administered and are easier to score and more difficult to challenge than other test instruments.

5. They provide the ability to rank-order candidates by numerical score.

6. They provide a permanent record of test performance that is available for review.

Predicting Future Successful Job Performance

Police promotional tests are often part achievement and part aptitude tests. An **achievement test** measures present proficiency, mastery and understanding of general and specific knowledge. An **aptitude test** predicts a candidate's capacity for achievement and competence.

All tests are an attempt to predict whether you have or will have the ability to perform at the next level—in other words, are you trainable?

How well the test functions as a predictor depends on to what extent the test is valid and reliable. Many police test-takers confuse promotional examinations with intelligence tests. Your IQ has little to do with the score you ultimately receive on a promotional test. That's not what the test is designed to measure.

Remember, your test will have questions relating to the knowledge, skills and abilities determined by those creating the exams to be essential in successfully performing the job. If you determine which duties a police detective performs most often and correlate them with the duties that are most important to be performed organizationally, you can make a good "guess estimate" about what you should be studying.

Don't spend a lot of time studying what a detective in a specialized division does if the majority of detectives in your department are generalists, for example. Know the broader points of specialization, but spend most of your time studying what's most likely to be on the test.

The Key to Success

Exceptional job performance, longevity, and superior intelligence have little to do with how well candidates perform on promotional tests. These characteristics are not what the test is designed to measure.

What really matters is

1. Self-motivation: how much you want to get promoted
2. Perseverance: how often and how well you study
3. Test-taking skills
4. Reading comprehension

I'm firmly convinced that the final ranking of the top 10% of candidates taking promotional examinations has more to do with individual motivation than with any other single criterion.

If thirty officers take a written test for detective, for example, the final rank order of at least the top 10% is often so closely spaced that there's no real difference in the test's predictive ability. Add the oral examination or an evaluation of training and experience to the written test mark, average the two, and the gaps between individuals widen considerably.

Here's a sample promotion list to further explain how this usually works:

Promotion List

Name	Written Exam	Oral Exam	Final Score
1. Robert Catania	96%	95%	92.5%
2. John Bowen	94%	90%	92.0%
3. Thomas Murray	91%	88%	89.5%
4. Peggy Clouser	90%	88%	89.0%
5. Rick Siena	87%	90%	88.5%
6. Michael Custer	84%	80%	82.0%
7. Hal Reed	90%	74%	82.0%
8. Edward Fuentes	81%	76%	78.5%
9. Susan Burns	78%	76%	77.0%
10. Phillip Cunningham	70%	80%	75.0%

The difference between the person who came out number one on this list with 95.5%, Catania, and the one who came out number five with 88.5%, Siena, is only seven points.

However, notice the widening gap as the list gets longer. The difference between number five with 88.5%, Siena, and number ten with 75.0%, Cunningham, is 13.5 points. The first four or five people on this particular list are so close that any of them could have come out number one. The only real difference between Catania and Siena is that Catania was, perhaps, more highly motivated, had better test-taking skills, and knew how to "play the game" better on the oral examination.

No one can really motivate another person to do anything—motivation must come from within. In studying for your promotional examinations, you're seeking advancement, a sense of achievement, status, and personal growth. No one can achieve their potential until they've set goals for themselves. To succeed, you must have a specific plan and the ability to motivate and consistently energize yourself toward a visualized goal. You need to establish the type of motivational climate that consistently pushes you towards your objectives. You're the only person who really knows what motivates you.

Galileo put it this way: "You cannot teach a man anything; you can only help him find it within himself." Create the vision and establish a plan to achieve your goal.

Since we were children, we've all used self-motivational techniques. Some become motivated by leafing through a notebook containing photographs and newspaper clippings highlighting their police careers. Others use family, the need for recognition or the pursuit of power. Whichever technique you use, make a contract with yourself, take a blood oath, develop a routine, master self-discipline, buy into the vision, and establish a plan of action.

The first step in establishing your plan of action is to resolve to take personal responsibility for your learning.

Consider the following:

- Setting clear goals is the foundation for success. Identify your learning objectives by developing a clear picture of what needs to happen, and take responsibility for achieving your goals. Develop a blueprint for success.

- List the critical success factors necessary to accomplish your goal. Commit to action. Ask yourself, What specific action could I take today that would help me achieve my goals? Work daily to improve your knowledge, skills and abilities.

- Apply concepts and techniques learned to your work environment.

- Establish an environment conducive to studying and learning.

- Remember that sweat rules over inspiration. There is no replacement for hard work, personal drive or ambition.

These simple steps will do more to assure that you do well on your tests than any other study aid.

Studying

By this time you'll have obtained all of the reference materials that were listed on the test announcement. A systematic approach to studying will pay you big dividends on test day. Arrange these books and other materials in a logical sequence grouped by subject matter. Place all of your department orders, procedures, training bulletins, state statutes, rules and regulations, etc., in order of declining importance by major topic area. Put this material into the three-ring notebooks you purchased. All of the job tasks associated with the rank you're testing for should be filed together and an index placed in front of each notebook. The test questions involving technical and procedural data specific to your department will come from this material. Place these notebooks aside. We'll come back to them later.

The books listed on the test announcement as references contain the generic information from which your test will be constructed. First, select the book that has the most content related to the index cards you've made out based on the major topic areas for the position for which you are testing: examples of duties and required knowledge, skills and abilities as listed in the test announcement.

Read the book, but make a deliberate effort to note key words and spend time reflecting on what the author is trying to tell you. At the end of each paragraph, cover the text with an index card and mentally ask yourself the following questions:

1. *What were the most important thoughts?*

2. *What is the author is trying to communicate to me?*

3. *Why is this section important? How does it relate to the other areas covered in this section?*

4. *How would a test question about this area be worded?*

Now, restructure the main ideas of the paragraph in your own words. As you're reading, use the dictionary to look up each word that you're not positive you know the meaning of. Write the definition on a sheet of paper. You'll better understand the ideas expressed if you compare them with your real-life police experiences. This procedure is called making a *positive mental transfer* and is discussed more fully later. Using this technique will improve both your reading comprehension and your vocabulary. Use this method to read the book a second time. The next step is more analytical.

Highlighting Material

On your third run-through, use a highlighter and go through the text, page by page, sentence by sentence, marking key words, phrases and sections.

a. Use a pink highlighter for any information that is particular to your department (procedural information found in your department's manuals, bulletins, etc.).

b. Use a yellow highlighter for books and other reference material listed on the test announcement (generic information).

c. Use a green highlighter for material found in other reference sources (this book, magazines, other police books, etc.).

Look for the important ideas and for terms the author uses repeatedly. Note the sometimes subtle changes in word meanings when they're used in different areas of policing. If the word or key phrase has several meanings, depending on how it's used, think about how the different concepts are related to one another. For instance, you might highlight sub-topics of obvious importance, such as the investigator's responsibilities at crime scenes. When in doubt, highlight it.

Once you've completed this task, begin writing all of the areas you've highlighted on separate index cards. Place a bold heading on the top of each card listing these topic areas. The reason this procedure works is that you learn by using your five senses. The more senses you stimulate while studying, the more likely you are to retain the information.

Studies show that about 75% of what we learn comes through the use of sight, and about 13% through hearing. We remember only about 30% of what we see and 20% of what we hear. Combining these two senses works out to a retention level of, at best, about 50%.

However, by using positive mental transfers in your studying process, you can greatly increase your ability to retain the principles and concepts on which you will be tested. Relate new material to a fact or experience you already know. For example, one of the definitions of the term ***corpus delicti*** is "establishing evidence that a criminal act has in fact occurred." Your study reference book may have large sections devoted to a variety of principles and concepts. However, to better retain the theories involved, relate investigation techniques to something within your own experience. You've undoubtedly been investigating criminal offenses and worked with detectives throughout your entire career. So you do know something about the subject that you can relate directly to the material you're studying. Create a mental picture of new study material that connects it to something familiar to you.

Repeating the Process

After you complete this procedure for the first book, repeat it for the rest of your reference material, including all the items you put into your three-ring binders.

Remember:

1. Read slowly, sentence by sentence.

2. Read for meaning and understanding.

3. Highlight key material.

4. Copy the highlighted material onto index cards.

While you're reading, don't allow your mind to wander. It's useless to move on to another topic unless you thoroughly understand the one you've just read. Slower comprehension often happens with technical material such as budgets or when studying graphs and charts. There's a big difference between being able to repeat a definition and understanding what it means. Always state the concept in your own words.

By the end of this procedure, you will have assembled an impressive stack of index cards divided into major topic areas and subdivided by specific classification. Time consuming? Yes. Boring, difficult, hard work? Yes. But it works.

Now, after assembling all your index cards, put a rubber band around each stack, dividing them by topic area. You'll carry them with you from now until test day. Every single free minute (in the car, while walking around, at lunch) read the cards until you know the material cold. Do this pick-up studying in addition to your planned sessions. You must master the subject matter to the extent that you can read the top of an index card (marked **Rigor Mortis**, for example) and, without looking, repeat what you had previously written. Continue doing this day in and day out, hour after hour.

Return to your reference material often, and reread constantly. Repetition improves memory. Understand key principles, know the theory behind topic areas, and study consistently. This is what it takes to come out number one. You only get one chance on a promotional test. After all, if it were easy, you wouldn't need superior motivation in order to succeed.

More Important Tips

1. Police promotional examinations are extremely competitive. Often, only tenths of a point separate the candidates and make the difference between promotion and failure. So don't study with others—they are your competition.

   While there are advantages to group study, such as feedback, any leverage you gain is offset by your helping people who'll be competing directly against you on test day. Study alone in a quiet setting for a minimum of two hours every day.

   It's difficult to study at home; there are too many interruptions, plus the constant temptation to take breaks. Two hours of study at a library, park or other quiet place is often better than four hours of study at home. Remember also to constantly write out the material while you're studying.

2. Don't procrastinate. It's easy to find reasons that may seem important at the time not to study. Schedule specific hours, and don't allow anything to interfere with your plans. If you're married, have a family meeting and explain what you're doing and your plans to accomplish it. Ask for you family's support, and try to involve them as much as possible in your goals.

3. Don't waste time studying what you already know. Most people have a tendency to study areas that are of specific interest to them or which they learn easily. Concentrate on the areas in which you are weakest.

4. During the week before the written test, rent a room in a quality hotel and move in for a couple of days to culminate your study efforts. I've done this before every promotional test I've taken and found it to be very beneficial. Schedule your time by allowing for several hours of intensive study followed by a break. During your breaks, eat, go for a swim, take a walk, or do whatever you find enjoyable. Then come back and hit the books again. Following is a suggested study schedule.

Hotel Study Schedule

DAY 1	
TIME	**ACTIVITY**
8am-9am	Breakfast
9am-11am	Study
11am-11:30am	Break
11:30am-12:30pm	Lunch
12:30pm-2:30pm	Study
2:30pm-3:30pm	Exercise
3:30pm-5:00pm	Study
5:00pm-6:00pm	Break
6:00pm-7:00pm	Study
7:00pm-8:00pm	Dinner
8:00pm-10:00pm	Study

DAY 2	
TIME	**ACTIVITY**
8:00am-9:00am	Breakfast
9:00am-12:00pm	Take Multiple Choice Practice Test #1
12:00pm-1:00pm	Lunch
1:00pm-1:30pm	Walk
1:30pm-3:30pm	Study areas of weakness as determined by Test #1
3:30pm-4:30pm	Exercise
4:30pm-7:30pm	Take Multiple Choice Practice Test#2
7:30pm-8:30pm	Dinner
8:30pm-10:00pm	Study areas of weakness as determined by Test #2

Note: While this schedule is a good, workable one, you may find that another arrangement works better for you. So don't treat it as the only appropriate way to use your study time. For example, you may find that taking Practice Test #1 a week or two before your hotel stay and spending more time on its result would be most helpful to you. What is important is that you have a schedule that suits you and that you stick to it.

If this seems like a lot of work to you, you're absolutely right. Promotion is very difficult to obtain because there are so many competitors vying for a limited number of vacancies. Lawyers studying for the bar exam can take their test again six months or a year later if they fail. You may have to wait three years or longer for another chance, so maximize your potential by doing everything necessary to ensure peak performance on test day.

Practice Test Taking

People who frequently take written examinations do better (all other factors excluded) than those who don't. If it has been several years since you last took a written test, practice as much as possible as part of your study routine. Taking sample tests will prove invaluable to you. Creating tests is easier than you may think. By this time, you should be able to construct some of your own question-and-answer selections. Creating your own test is an effective way to study. Just make sure you're positive of the right answers.

Taking the Multiple Choice Test

Bring the following with you on test day:

1. A tape recorder

2. A box of paper clips

3. Several No. 2 pencils

4. A durable eraser

5. A large pad of paper

6. A watch

Your Physical Condition

Get a good night's rest before taking the test. This is one of the most important days of your career, so don't make the mistake of staying up late the night before the exam. If you wear glasses, don't forget to bring them. Dress comfortably. You won't be graded for your appearance on the written examination.

The Directions

When you arrive at the test site, choose a seat in the front row where you can hear the test directions better and where you'll have fewer distractions. Listen carefully to the test proctor. Use your tape recorder to record the oral directions given for taking the exam (especially if comments are being made about how to challenge specific questions). Sometimes the "rules" are changed at the last minute and suddenly announced on test day, particularly in matters relating to grading the test or to the relative weights of test sections.

If the method is different from that listed in the examination announcement and you don't feel the change is beneficial to you, immediately notify the exam proctor and file an objection. Silence means acceptance. The test won't be stopped just because you file a protest, but you will have established the groundwork for later appeals.

Time

You'll be told exactly how much time you have in which to take the test. Quickly review all parts of the test to estimate how much time it will take you to complete it.

A minute and a half per question on a 100-question multiple-choice exam would take 150 minutes (two and a half hours) to complete. In a three-hour test, that would leave only thirty minutes for review. Check the time frequently to be sure you're on schedule.

The Test Booklet and Answer Sheet

Read the instructions in the test booklet carefully. If there's something you don't understand, ask!

Be sure that you have all the test materials that the oral and written instructions indicate that you should have. Usually, computer-type answer sheets are used for promotional examinations.

Follow the oral and written directions and use the type of pencil indicated by the exam proctor. Fill in your answers completely, and don't make any notations or marks on the answer sheet that might confuse the computer into taking points away from you.

Understanding Questions and Answers

Before you begin the written test, ask the exam proctor whether you're allowed to mark on the test booklet.

If you are, use this procedure to increase your comprehension of the questions and answer selections:

1. Carefully read the question and circle each word you don't know the definition of or are confused about. You can usually get a good idea of what the word means by reading the entire section.

2. Go back to the word you circled and substitute another word that you feel more comfortable with. Use this same process for the selection choices.

If the test proctor will not allow writing in the exam booklet, which sometimes is the case, write the confusing terms on a separate piece of paper.

Marking Questions and Answers

When taking the test, if you're allowed to write in the test booklet, highlight or underline key words in both the question and the answer selections.

If you come to a question you're not sure of, skip it, but do one of two things so that you can quickly return to the question later:

Either

1. Put a paper clip alongside the number of the question on both the test booklet and the answer sheet.

Or

2. Put a check mark next to the number of the question on both the test booklet and the answer sheet. If you use this method, be sure that you completely erase all the check marks from the answer sheet before time is called so that the computer doesn't identify them as wrong answers.

In almost every police examination, someone skips a question and then gets his or her answer sheet out of sequence, resulting in a very low score. Using the paper clips or check marks will help you avoid this disaster.

As you read the questions, circle the correct answer in the booklet and then transfer your selection to the answer sheet. In most multiple choice tests, there are four or five answer selections. You can usually eliminate two of the answers as being obviously wrong. If it's allowed, cross them out in the examination booklet. In a four-question selection spread, you've increased your odds, if randomly selecting the answer, from one in four to one in two. You now have to select only the best answer of the remaining two answers. Make certain you understand what the question is asking.

Many answer selections contain words called *specific determiners*. Specific determiners that are too broad often indicate the wrong choice.

Examples of broad specific determiners are

only, all, never, nothing, everyone, no, always, none, must

Words that often indicate the correct answer are

could, might, can, usually, sometimes, any, often, generally, frequently, occasionally, possibly, rarely, normally, seldom, some

Above all, make sure that you don't get stuck on any one question. Remember, all the questions have the same value, so if you hit a question that seems very complex or very difficult, mark it, fill in a "guess" answer, and move on. There's no point in agonizing over it and wasting your valuable time or letting it throw you so completely that you lose concentration on following questions.

Returning to Unanswered Questions

Never leave questions unanswered unless the oral or written instructions indicate that you don't lose credit for questions left blank. Often, as you're taking the test, another question will refresh your memory about one of the questions that you've taken a guess on. Then you need merely go back to the questions you've paper clipped or check marked and select the right answer.

If this isn't the case, carefully reread the questions, circling key words and phrases and substituting your own words in questions and answers. The most difficult questions often leave you with two answer alternatives that are often in direct conflict with one another (an either-or situation), yet both seem somehow to be correct. If you're stuck, stay with your best guess.

Changing Answers

It seems that every time I've taken a test and changed an answer, I invariably changed a correct answer to an incorrect one. Test-taking statistics indicate that this is most often the case. Unless you're positive that the revised selection is correct, don't change your answers. ***Trust your initial instincts.***

If you do change an answer, make certain to completely erase the original answer mark. Be sure, too, to review all of your answers if you have time remaining at the end of the test, to be certain that you haven't carelessly filled in a wrong answer choice even though you know the right answer. It can happen, so double check. Above all, make sure that you don't get stuck on any one question. Remember, all the questions have the same point value, so if you hit a question that seems very confusing, return to it later.

Multiple-Choice Practice Tests

The content of the written examination for detective within police organizations varies from department to department. However, the theories and concepts involved remain constant. It doesn't matter whether you work in Los

Angeles, California, or Rutland, Vermont, when it comes to criminal investigation. The general principles of what an investigator should do are the same.

Multiple-choice practice tests are representative and deal with broad-based investigative concepts, principles, and theory common to all police departments. The object in taking practice examinations is twofold—first, to enable you to assess your strengths and weaknesses so that you will know which areas to give further attention to; second, to increase your skill in test taking. People who practice taking tests do better, all other factors excluded, on their examinations.

Before you take the practice multiple-choice examinations, reread the sections on improving your techniques for taking multiple-choice examinations Make the conditions in which you take the practice tests as realistic as possible.

Find a quiet place, free from interruptions. Follow the directions carefully. Use a standard computer-type answer sheet (the vast majority of written examinations use them).

Take the entire exam in one sitting and in the time allotted, without using any references. Manage your time and highlight key words in the questions and answer selections.

Don't read information into the questions that is not there or change your answers unless you're positive. Experiment with the test booklet by marking out answer selections as they are eliminated, etc.

After finishing the test, compare your selections with the answer key. Answers and analysis follow each practice test. Be sure to read all of these.

Good luck!

Chapter Ten

The Oral Examination

Most cities use some form of oral examination as part of the promotional testing process for the position of detective in a police department. In fact, oral tests are used more than any other evaluation instrument to "predict" the future ability of people to successfully perform the job at the next level. It's also the type of test police officers spend the least amount of time preparing for, even though they have a more personal control over the outcome of this type of testing than any other, with the possible exception of assessment centers.

In many cities, the oral examination counts for up to 50% of a candidate's final average score. Other cities assign a "weight" to the scores on the written and oral examination and add points for seniority, performance evaluations, police training and experience, etc.

Receiving a high score on the oral examination depends largely on three things:

1. Your understanding of the framework involved in constructing and conducting oral examinations.

2. How well and which method you use to prepare for the test. Your score will ultimately depend on how much time and effort you put into preparing for the examination.

3. Your performance on test day. As in the world of sports, it's what you do today that counts. Your past performance, the fact that you received the department's medal of honor or that you were named the nation's police officer of the year won't matter if you can't verbally communicate the right answers to the questions on test day.

The Difference Between Oral and Written Tests

A promotional test is a systematic process to identify normal expectations of acceptable proficiency at the level the test is designed to measure. The written examination is designed to test your ability to apply analytical thinking, demonstrate practical judgment, analyze facts and use deductive reasoning to prioritize. At the investigative level, it measures proficiency, mastery and understanding of general (generic) and specific (procedural) job knowledge.

The oral examination is designed to measure desirable qualities as well as knowledge, skills and abilities that the written examination cannot test. What the written test lacks is the ability to accurately evaluate your intrinsic qualities—such as leadership potential or organizational integrity.

Written tests are incapable of recognizing ***doing behaviors***, such as verbal communication skills or appearance. Doing behaviors are a combination of verbal responses, body language, gestures and appearance factors that are observable to those administering the examination.

Oral examinations provide the tester the opportunity to do the following:

1. Meet the candidate face-to-face and ask open-ended, role-playing questions.

2. Ask questions that investigate and probe the content and reasoning behind a candidate's answers.

3. Determine a candidate's beliefs, attitudes, maturity, intentions and depth of understanding.

4. Observe a candidate's lack of knowledge or confusion in specific areas.

5. Observe whether a candidate does or does not possess a wide range of qualities—for example, stable behavior, ethics, and personal integrity.

You can exercise a great deal of control over your score in the oral examination. Knowing how these tests are constructed and the process used to conduct and grade the oral examination will help you prepare for the test.

The Oral Board

An oral board is a testing process used to assess and rank-order candidates according to abilities that have been predetermined to be necessary for successful job performance. Because of heavy litigation in the promotional testing process, personnel analysts often go to great lengths to ensure that the oral examination is conducted in an objective, or fair, manner.

To avoid claims of personal bias or favoritism, subject matter experts from outside your department will serve as panelists on your oral board. Typical oral boards have three panel members. If there are many applicants, several boards may be convened, with each handling a fraction of the pool of candidates. Each board will ask exactly the same questions and use the same criteria to grade their candidates.

There is a trend to further diversify panels by including civilian police representatives. In addition to officers from other cities, civilian police analysts, police psychologists, city managers and deputy city managers or other non-sworn personnel are asked to participate in the oral examination. Oral boards testing for the position of police detective are normally sergeants and above.

The oral panel can convene in any facility large enough to accommodate a long conference table and four or five chairs. It should not be located in your own police department.

The oral board is often held at a city hall, a local high school or college, or another government building in your community. Candidates who successfully pass the written examination (the cutoff score is usually 70%) are notified by mail of their score and the date, time, and location at which they've been scheduled to appear before the oral board.

The letter announcing your oral board date usually contains a number or coded device that you're required to bring with you to the exam.

The people chosen to be on your oral panel may have a great deal of experience serving on oral boards, or they may have very little. None of them will be professional interviewers.

Regardless of who is chosen to be on the board, they will have received material from your city's personnel department containing the following information:

1. The position description.

2. An organizational chart of your police department.

3. The procedure to be used to conduct the oral examination.

4. Interview techniques and instructions.

5. Instructions on how to rate and score the candidates.

The Position Description

Although the primary duties and responsibilities of police detectives are similar across the country, different departments may emphasize some job tasks more than others. For example, a large city police department may find some job tasks, knowledge or skills important that would be relatively unimportant in a small town.

For this reason, it is vital that you have the ***position description*** (also called the job description) for the job for which you are applying. Panelists and/or test administrators use the position description as a guide in formulating the questions they'll ask you at the oral board. They want to be sure that the questions are both appropriate and related to the job performed by people currently in the position you're testing for.

Conducting the Oral Examination

In some cities, oral board panelists attend a class on the various aspects of conducting the oral examination. Other cities merely have the people who have been selected arrive several hours before the first candidate to receive a briefing on the oral examination procedure used by your city. The meeting is usually conducted by the test administrator assigned to oversee the process. During that time, the panelists get to know each other and review the questions they'll ask the candidates at the oral examination.

Most cities allow panelists to construct their own test questions, although the city reviews them to make sure they are both appropriate and job related. Inappropriate or illegal questions are discarded. Areas that must be avoided include race, color, national origin, ancestry, age, marital status, political party membership or activities, religious affiliation or church attendance.

In addition to the legal ramifications of improper questions is an awareness that candidates might be upgraded or downgraded because of a panelist's personal bias. For this reason, some cites create their own mandatory and optional questions and divide them among the panelists to ask candidates at the interviews.

The oral examination questions are designed to impartially and objectively evaluate the knowledge, skills and aptitude of each candidate and to rank the candidates in order of their competence. It's the panelists' responsibility to rate the candidates' responses and rate them objectively.

Because the board has only a short time to spend with each candidate (from twenty to forty-five minutes, depending on how many candidates are to be interviewed), they can ask only a limited number of questions. Each panelist selects two or three questions, which then become the mandatory questions. Each candidate must be asked the mandatory questions; however, the panelists are free to ask optional or follow-up questions, and they frequently do.

During this preliminary meeting, the panelists are asked to review a list containing the names and addresses of each candidate to make sure they don't know any of the candidates personally. If a panelist does know an individual on the list, the test administrator may decide to excuse that board member from interviewing that particular candidate, and the administrator fills in for the panelist.

During the meeting, one of the panelists or the test administrator is elected to greet each candidate and introduce him or her to the others. There will be a tape recorder in the room which will be operated by either a panel member or the test administrator. Another panelist or the test administrator acts as a timekeeper to ensure that each candidate has approximately the same amount of time with the oral board.

Scoring the Examination

The purpose of the oral examination is to measure a candidate's intrinsic qualities, which the written test can't adequately evaluate. In order to reduce the subjective nature of this type of process, a rating device is created that limits factors being tested for so the range of scores isn't so wide that the test becomes invalid or unreliable. Following are samples of rating forms commonly used to evaluate candidates for management ranks within police departments.

Sample Rating Form

DETECTIVE CANDIDATE RATING FORM

Name/Number: _____   Final Score: _____

Rating Factors/Dimensions

1. Oral Communication Skills
Demonstrated ability to speak clearly and precisely. Ability   _____
to use appropriate interpersonal communication styles and
language to fit the situation. Clarity of expression.

2. Appearance, Manner and Bearing
General appearance, enthusiasm, mannerisms, posture,   _____
body language. Will this candidate's appearance help
him or her in the job of police detective?

3. Responsibility, Maturity
Possession of maturity necessary to handle the responsibilities   _____
of a police detective. Possession of integrity required of the
position, awareness of the seriousness of the position.

4. Job Knowledge
Thorough understanding of the duties, necessary abilities,   _____
methods, and practices of the position and ability to learn
and use proper skills in the performance of duties.

5. Interest, Attitude
Genuine interest in the position sought. Positive attitude about   _____
the functions of a police detective.

6. Alertness, Self-Confidence
Readiness in grasping the meaning of questions, demonstrated   _____
self-confidence, surety of answers. Ability to present ideas in a
logical, coherent fashion. Displays vigor, initiative and drive.

7. Judgment/Problem Solving   _____
Ability to exercise good judgment, make decisions, dependability,
consistency, use logic, get to the root of the problem, weigh
alternatives, analyze, come to conclusions, separate the important
from the unimportant.

8. Working Relationships, Adaptability   _____
Ability to manage stress, promote worker cooperation, adapt
to the changing nature of the position. Displays confidence,
tact and sensitivity in dealing with others.

9. Organizational Integrity   _____
Willingness to put department goals ahead of personal goals.

10. Overall Impression   _____
General appearance, communication skills, enthusiasm,
mannerisms, clarity of expression, judgment and self-confidence.

Panel #: _____ / **Panelist Signature:** _____

The criteria established in the preliminary meeting, the rating form used by your city and the predetermined questions selected to be used on the oral examination comprise the test process by which candidates are evaluated. During your oral examination, three panelists will take notes on your performance. Immediately after you leave, each panelist privately reviews his or her notes and assigns a numerical rating to each of the categories. After the panelists' individual ratings are completed, they discuss any significant differences between their ratings. One or more of the panelists may have observed some performance, positive or negative, that was overlooked by another.

The board members don't have to reach a consensus, however, and they are not encouraged to alter their ratings unless they are convinced their preliminary scoring was off. After the board members have thoroughly reviewed your ratings, they total and average the scores and assign a final score, which is your oral examination mark.

First Impression—Lasting Impression

The impression you make with the oral board in the first few minutes is critical. The oral board is an opportunity to sell yourself. You never get a second chance to make a good first impression. The oral panel will begin forming an impression about you based on what they see, what you say and how you say it. The moment you enter the room, you're on center stage, and the panelists will be influenced by everything about you, either positively or negatively.

The image you project to the panelists depends largely on

- How you walk into and out of the room.

- Your posture.

- Your appearance.

- Your speech and its tonal qualities.

- Your body movements and gestures.

- The words you choose and how you say them.

- Your facial expressions.

- The amount and intensity of eye contact with the panel.

All of these factors communicate information about you to the panel. You must be able to communicate your best and strongest traits with confidence, energy and enthusiasm. Most accomplished speakers spend hours practicing before they get up in front of an audience. The more you rehearse, the better you'll perform on test day. If your appearance, body language and mannerisms are appropriate, the panel will be free to concentrate on what you are saying.

Preparing for Your Oral Examination

Now that you have a basic understanding of how the oral board works, you can prepare a method to study for the examination. In most departments, it takes from three to six weeks to correct the written examination and announce the results to candidates. Use the time between the written examination and the oral test to your advantage.

Don't wait to receive your written test score to begin studying for the oral examination. In order to succeed, start studying again the day after the written test and continue until the moment you walk into the room to take your oral exam.

To achieve high scores in any oral interview, you must have excellent verbal communication skills. Clear and effective communication (including body language) is the manner in which you transmit information about yourself to the panelists. Knowledge is not enough in an oral exam. You must orally communicate what you know and explain how you will use that knowledge as a police detective.

The test questions are designed to place you in hypothetical situations in which you must make a decision to

1. Take a particular course of action as a detective.

2. Accomplish an investigative task (delegate).

Because the exam responses are oral, you must be able to communicate to he panel members in a clear, concise, understandable manner. One reason that officers fail oral examinations is their tendency to answer questions by indicating what they would do at their current level, rather than at the level at which they are testing for.

Questions relating to the following areas require responses at the detective, not the officer, level:

How you would go about...

  — managing a crime scene?

  — taking written statements, preparing affidavits and search warrants?

  — conducting follow-up investigations?

  — investigating specific crimes, such as murder, rape, burglary and assault?

  — asking legal questions relative to constitutional law, search and seizure, Miranda, and arrest?

  — processing forensics and evidence?

In studying for the oral examination, you must know the terms, concepts, and specific processes associated with both generic and procedural investigations in your department. When studying for the written examination, you read the reference material several times, highlighted areas, wrote out the subject matter on legal pads and index cards, and committed the information to memory.

However, because the exam responses will be oral, to prepare effectively, you must practice speaking these concepts and definitions out loud. Knowing all of the material is not enough; you must be able to communicate that knowledge in a clear, concise and understandable manner to the panelists. If the information remains locked in your head and never comes out of your mouth, or does so haltingly, you've lost the opportunity to tell the board what you know.

Techniques to Improve Your Verbal Communication Skills

1. Review the major topic areas, investigative dimensions, concepts and subjects you placed on your index cards for the written examination.

2. Correlate these with the "Glossary of Key Terms" in the back of this book.

3. Begin creating your own oral board questions on a new set of index cards and follow each with the correct response that you derive from your resource material.

For instance, in making up your questions, you might develop one like this:

"How can DNA analysis be used in a criminal investigation?"

Or a question such as this one:

"Under what circumstances can a detective search a person, place or thing without a search and seizure warrant?"

The panel assumes you know the textbook definitions to these questions, but remember, the board isn't judging you on technical job knowledge. It's judging you but on such criteria as communication skills, attitude, judgment and maturity.

Use the questions to showcase the skills for which you are being tested. Yes, show the board that you know the book definitions and concepts involved, but also give specific explanations of how you would use leadership, motivational, interpersonal and management skills to successfully handle the situation you've outlined.

Creating Your Own Mock Oral Board

Pretend that you're actually at the oral board, and use the tape recorder you bought to practice answering the questions you develop. Play the tape back and put yourself in the position of a panelist judging your answer. Does the answer indicate knowledge and understanding beyond the basic question? Does it show your ability to apply investigative theories and concepts? Are your thoughts well organized? How would you rate your communication skills? Do they flow easily, or are your main points disjointed and confused with *uh*'s and *ah*'s and gaps between ideas? Do you say *"you know"* over and over again?

Create an oral board in your own home. Tape ten or fifteen of the questions you created. Space the questions with approximately five minutes of blank tape between them. Get a table and place three chairs behind it. Put a pad and pencil in front of each chair. You now have created your own mock oral panel. Set a fourth chair in front of the table and put your tape recorder on the table in front of it. Practice entering the room and seating yourself in front of the panel. Turn on the tape recorder and begin your first question.

The first question in the oral board process is usually an icebreaker, designed to put the candidate at ease. It might be, "Before we begin the formal test process, please tell the board about yourself." Answer the question exactly as you would at a real oral board. Continue through all of the questions and repeat this process until you get it perfect.

Another technique is to have your spouse, a friend or a family member ask you the questions so you can practice your responses. Rent a video camera to photograph your practice sessions so you can see yourself as others see you.

Watch closely to see whether you're engaging in ***image distortion***. Image distortion occurs when your words say one thing, but your posture, gestures, and voice inflections say something else. You create an image different from the one you think you are creating.

When reviewing the video, ask yourself the following questions.

1. *What do I look like? Am I crossing my arms over my chest in a closed, protective position?*

2. *What do I sound like?*

3. *Am I sitting properly? Am I fidgeting in my seat or the arms of the chair tightly?*

4. *Are my facial expressions and gestures appropriate for an oral test? Are my gestures artificial?*

5. *Do I make eye contact with all three panel members when answering the questions?*

You may be surprised, after reviewing the video, to discover that you have more weak points than you realized. Seeing yourself as others see you and adjusting for weaknesses is a very positive practice tool. At first, you may feel awkward answering questions at your mock oral board, but you'll quickly see a vast improvement in your performance. Be sure to use all the oral exam practice material contained in this chapter.

Your Physical Appearance and Other Significant Factors

In addition to thorough knowledge of the resource material and excellent verbal communication skills, many other factors also weigh heavily in the oral examination process. From the moment the panelists or test administrator comes out to the waiting room to get you, you're being judged. The panel has about thirty minutes to make a decision relative to your score. Your facial expressions, gestures, hair style, clothing, and how you walk, smile and talk all have an impact on what your final grade will be. Board members will consciously or subconsciously judge you on many of the following items.

The Police Uniform

Even though this is a detective examination, in some cities and towns, you will be required to wear your police uniform to the test. Bring an extra uniform in your car on the day of the test in case you have an unfortunate mishap on the way there. It's also a good idea to bring a sticky lint roller with you and a handkerchief to touch up the shine on you shoes just before you go into your oral examination.

The Police Hat

If you're appearing before the oral board in uniform, have your police hat with you. If yours is soiled or has lost its shape, get a new one. Shine both the hat's bill and the cap device, or its shield, to a high gloss. If it's a winter hat, make sure it's free of lint. Wear your hat when you enter the room, salute if appropriate, take the hat off and put it under your left arm before you sit down, and then place it beneath your chair.

This maneuver takes a little practice before it's smooth and military. When the exam is over, the panelists will all and offer to shake your hand. Shake hands firmly, then put your hat back on before you leave. The panelists will be looking at your back as you exit, so square your shoulders and walk erectly.

Uniform Shirt

Unless you're required to, do not wear a uniform coat or jacket; they're bulky and prevent freedom of movement. Whether you're in long sleeves or short, make sure all of the little threads are removed from around the buttons of your uniform shirt pockets.

The shirt should be spotless, have a noticeable crease along the sleeve, and be completely free from lint both front and back. If military creases are not sewn in, ask your cleaner to iron them in. Display your shield, name tag, issued insignia and medals according to your department regulations.

Uniform Tie

Wear the authorized tie. It must be clean and wrinkle- and lint-free. Its clasp should be department issue and properly placed.

Uniform Trousers

Make sure that your police trousers fit properly, especially at the shoe line, and that they have a razor-sharp, military crease. The front and back of the pants must be free of lint.

Don't put anything in your pockets—remove your wallet, keys, and loose change. You don't want to jingle when you enter or leave the room or have any unnecessary bulges that take away from a streamlined, military appearance.

Gun Belt

Unless your gun belt is already highly polished and free of cracks, buy a new one and polish it up, paying particular attention to the buckle. Shine your holster too. If it's showing signs of wear, get a replacement.

If your service weapon has wooden grips, polish them as well, and clean the weapon itself, especially the part that protrudes from the holster.

Clean your handcuffs and wear them as your department requires (in a case or hanging by a strap). If you're allowed to use a case, do so to avoid having them rattle when you enter the room, sit down and leave.

Don't bring your police radio or nightstick with you, and obviously, don't bring any unauthorized devices.

Insignias

Office department insignias (firearms expert, etc.) may be worn, but do not wear any insignia that is not issued and/or authorized by your department.

Name Tag

Unless you're instructed otherwise, wear your name tag in accordance with your department regulations.

Police Shield

Polish it to a high gloss.

Shoes

Wear laced black shoes that can be shined to a high gloss, including the heels and edges of the shoes.

Socks

Wear new, clean, black socks.

Medals

If you've received a department citation or been awarded a medal, wear it.

Hair

Get a haircut before the oral exam. Your hair should be neat and well trimmed, and its length should conform to any requirements outlined in your department's rules and regulations. Female officers should style their hair to reflect departmental standards, yet maintain their femininity.

Facial Hair

Even if your department permits beards, shave yours off. Mustaches and sideburns must also conform to your department's regulations.

Earrings

Under no circumstances should a male officer wear an earring to an oral test. If you usually do wear an earring, allow enough time for the hole to be unnoticeable before the oral board. Women should make sure their earrings are small and appropriate for work; dangling earrings call attention to themselves, not to your responses to the questions.

Fingernails

Your fingernails should clean and trimmed. Women should avoid long nails and colored polish; short nails with no polish or a clear gloss would be best.

Rings

If you have a college ring, by all means, wear it. If you're married, wear your wedding band. For women, sparkling diamond rings, especially ones that stick up above the hand, are best left at home. Don't wear more than one ring on each hand. Pinkie rings are not appropriate for men or women.

Make-Up

Most female police officers wear little make-up or none at all, so it's best to keep make-up to a minimum.

Business Attire

If you're directed not to wear your police uniform to the oral examination, dress conservatively. Men should wear a dark blue or gray suit. Women should wear a conservatively styled and colored business suit with skin-colored nylon stockings. Suits should be fresh from the cleaners and free of lint, both front and back. Men's trousers should be sharply creased and fit properly at the shoe line. Don't put anything in your pockets. Women should not carry a purse.

Men's belts, shoes, socks and ties should match their suits. The tie must be wrinkle-free and neatly knotted. Do not wear a tie clasp. A starched, white, long-sleeved shirt should be worn, regardless of the season. Both men's and women's shoes must be spotless and highly shined. Women should wear low-heeled shoes.

Tips

When you find out where the oral board will be located, drive over and see what the parking situation is. Will you have to walk several blocks? You'll have to allow time for that. What if it rains or snows and makes a mess out of your uniform? Plan for that too; be sure you have an extra uniform to leave in your car, and bring an umbrella along with your change of clothes.

Pack a shaving case with a hairbrush, lint roller, handkerchief, and nail file. Put it into a gym bag along with your hat and polished shoes and bring it with you. Find a bathroom and make certain you're squared away before your name or number is called. Try not to let other candidates present "psych" you out. Mentally get yourself ready.

Checklists

Post the following checklists at home, and make sure you've taken care of each item before you leave for the test.

Male Checklist

Business Attire   ☐

Attendance card or code number   ☐

Beard (shave)   ☐

Belt (to match suit) ☐

College ring/wedding band ☐

Comb ☐

Handkerchief (for shoes) ☐

Fingernails (clean and trim) ☐

Gas (fill up car) ☐

Gym bag or carrying case ☐

Hairbrush ☐

Haircut ☐

Know what time the test is ☐

Know where to go ☐

Know where to park ☐

Leave early ☐

Lint roller ☐

Money ☐

Nail file ☐

Shirt (white, long-sleeved, starched) ☐

Shoes (to match suit, cleaned and polished) ☐

Socks (to match shoes and suit) ☐

Suit (dark gray or blue) ☐

Trousers (military creases) ☐

Female Checklist

Attendance card or code number   ☐

College ring/wedding band   ☐

Comb   ☐

Handkerchief for shoes   ☐

Earrings (appropriate for a business meeting)   ☐

Fingernails (clean, clear polish)   ☐

Gas (fill up car)   ☐

Gym bag or carrying case   ☐

Hair (style appropriate for a business meeting)   ☐

Hairbrush   ☐

Know what time the test is   ☐

Know where to go   ☐

Know where to park   ☐

Leave early   ☐

Lint roller   ☐

Make-up (appropriate for a business meeting)   ☐

Money   ☐

Nail file   ☐

Shoes (to match suit, clean and polished)   ☐

Suit (appropriate for a business meeting)   ☐

Police Uniform Checklist
Male or Female

Badge (shine)   ☐

Extra uniform (take with you)   ☐

Gun (clean, polish wooden grips)   ☐

Gun, belt, and holster (shine)   ☐

Hat (shine bill, lint free)   ☐

Name tag (wear, unless instructed otherwise)   ☐

Official Insignia (wear)   ☐

Shirt (trim threads, military creases, lint-free)   ☐

Shoes (black, laced, highly polished)   ☐

Tie (authorized, clean, wrinkle-free)   ☐

Trousers (military creases, lint-free)   ☐

Questions Frequently Asked on Oral Boards

The questions asked on oral examinations for the position of detective vary across the country. However, in most cases, the initial question may provide you with the opportunity to communicate to the board information about yourself that can have a dramatic impact on your final score.

Often the first question is some type of icebreaker designed to put you at ease, such as, "Tell us about yourself and what you have done to prepare for the position of police detective."

The point is that this is something you can take definite steps to prepare for. Get out a legal pad and write out a four-minute opening statement. What makes you different from the other candidates walking in the door? Do you have a college degree? Are you currently attending college? What schools and seminars has the department sent you to? Why are they relevant to the position of detective? Which medals and/or citations have you been awarded? How long have you been on the job? Which assignments prepared you for the position of detective: Patrol? A stint in investigations? Undercover work? Specialized Units? Search warrants? Big cases solved? Crime scene experience? Forensic experience? Informants? Do you live in the city? Did you attend school in the city? Why would this be important in being a detective?

Ask them for the job. Tell them this is your dream. Tell the board you will be the best detective the city has ever had. If you don't, some other candidate will.

The ability to communicate is considered a requisite for the position of police detective. After all, it's an *oral board*, and the ability to communicate is a large part of the testing process. So practice your opening statement. It may make the difference in whether or not you get promoted.

The following questions represent broad subject areas and principles of police investigations that frequently appear on oral examinations. You may have to adjust your answer to suit your organization's circumstances.

1. ***Tell us about yourself and what you have done to prepare for the position of police detective.***

Possible Response:

As mentioned previously, this is your opportunity to communicate to the board what makes you special. The board can grade only what they see and hear. Start with high school and proceed to the present. Explain to the board why what you're telling them is relevant to your being a police detective. Stress education, training, job experience, time on the job, special abilities, enthusiasm, love of the department and excellent communication skills.

---

2. ***You are presenting a photographic array that includes a 22-year-old white suspect to three witnesses. What steps would you take to make certain the methodology you use to show the photographs will be admissible in court?***

Possible Response:

The key to using photographic displays is to ensure that the procedure doesn't suggest to a victim or witness that a particular photograph among those shown represents a suspect in the case. To meet any legal challenge to an identification of a suspect using this method, there are several steps I would take.

First of all, I would put the witnesses in three separate rooms and not allow them to see other witnesses participating in the viewing of the photographs in the array. They should not be allowed to communicate with one another until after the entire procedure is completed. It's always best to have another officer present during the entire procedure.

At least eight photographs must be in the display, and all of the photographs must be of people of the same race and approximate age and reasonably resemble the suspect. Colored photographs should not be mixed with black-and-white photographs, and all identifying numbers or letters must be removed from the photographs prior to any witness of victim viewing them.

Nothing in the photograph should suggest to the witness that the suspect committed the crime, and I must make certain that I do not suggest or imply that a particular suspect is in the photographic display. If a witness identifies a photograph in the array, the witness will sign the photograph identified and initial all of the other photographs in the array.

All of the photographs would be kept together, a detailed report written, and all the photos in the display placed in an evidence envelope and properly submitted to the evidence room. I would obtain a receipt and staple the receipt to the report. I would keep a copy of the report and the evidence receipt in my own files of the case.

I would be mindful that, even when an identification is made of a particular photograph, studies have shown that this type of identification procedure is not as reliable as scientific, forensic evidence. However, if all three witnesses picked out the same photograph of the suspect in the case, I would feel more confident moving forward and conducting an interview with the suspect if he/she could be located and/or applying for an arrest warrant.

I believe that if I took the steps I've outlined, any identification of a suspect in the photographic display would be allowed at a subsequent judicial proceeding.

----

3. *You are investigating a robbery of a purse in which the suspect displayed a handgun. A short time after the robbery, patrol officers arrested a suspect and found the victim's credit cards in the suspect's pockets. However, the victim states she had $500 in her purse, but the suspect has no cash nor a gun on his person. The suspect lives in his aunt's home, a short distance from where patrol arrested him. He does not pay rent. The aunt gives you permission to search his room. Would you search the room or obtain a search and seizure warrant to search the house?*

Possible Response:

One of the exceptions to the requirement that the police obtain a search warrant prior to searching a person's home is consent. I could have the aunt sign a form giving me consent to search the room and have the form witnessed by an impartial person. However, since the suspect is in custody and the aunt is being cooperative, I see no reason to hurry.

Consent searches, even with a form signed, give rise to claims that the consent was not intelligent or informed. It could also be later argued in court that the consent was coerced in some manner.

There is also the matter of the room. The aunt may be willing to have her nephew's room searched, but not her own. So, I would prefer to have officers stay at the premises and obtain a search and seizure warrant so I could search the entire home for the weapon and cash.

I believe that this would mitigate any of the adverse claims I've discussed and be more likely to withstand any Exclusionary Rule argument made by defense counsel.

---

4. *A woman has been sexually assaulted. After several weeks of investigation, you develop a suspect in the case and ask him to come to police headquarters to be interviewed. He drives his own car to headquarters and is there voluntarily. You advise the suspect he is free to leave at any time. Are you required to read the suspect his Miranda rights? Even if you aren't required to read the suspect his rights, would you do so anyway?*

Possible Response:

The courts have repeatedly ruled that *Miranda v. Arizona* is a two-pronged test requiring both custody and interrogation. If a person is not in custody, then the person doesn't have to be given their Fifth Amendment Miranda rights.

You have outlined a classic case in which the courts have ruled Miranda is not required. The suspect came to the station voluntarily and was told he was free to leave at any time. However, the onus is on the police to demonstrate that the suspect was not coerced to come to the station and was in fact free to leave. That's a very heavy burden to overcome if the suspect does in fact admit to committing a crime. The question is going to be why he would voluntarily come to the station and admit to committing a crime.

So I would read him his Miranda rights in the presence of another officer and have him sign a rights form even though it could be argued that technically I am not required to. I believe an investigator has to look beyond the moment and think about how the legal ramifications will play out in a court trial.

---

5. What is "probable cause"?

Possible Response:

The Fourth Amendment to the United States Constitution states that people have a right to be secure in their persons, houses, papers and effects against unreasonable searches and seizures, and no warrants shall issue, but upon probable cause supported by oath or affirmation, and particularly describing the place to be searched, and the persons or things to be seized.

In order for a police officer to make an "arrest"—with or without an arrest warrant signed by a judge —the officer must be able to conclude to a reasonable probability that an offense has been committed and that probable cause exists to believe the person is in fact a criminal participant.

Probable cause requires a higher standard than reasonable suspicion, but less than the standard of proof of beyond a reasonable doubt, which is required for conviction in court. Probable cause is a series of facts and circumstances—a step-by-step progression—which, by themselves or in combination, may be used by a reasonably prudent person to believe that a crime was committed and the suspect to be arrested committed the crime.

---

6. A suspect is arrested for Breach of Peace outside a local bar. At the time of his arrest, the suspect was sitting behind the wheel of his car. The arresting officer observed the handle of a gun sticking out from under the front seat. The officer seizes a .45 automatic and charges the suspect, who does not have a permit, with possession of the weapon. Discuss whether or not this is a legal search.

Possible Response:

As I mentioned earlier, there are seven exceptions to the requirement that officers have a search and seizure warrant signed by a judge prior to searching a person, place or thing. One of those exceptions is *plain view*.

The United States Supreme Court ruled in 1990 in *Horton v. California* that when an officer has a right to be where he or she is, anything an officer observes in plain view is not the product of a search and is admissible as evidence. If the police have probable cause to believe something observed is contraband, stolen property or other evidence of a crime, the police can seize it if they are lawfully in a place and see it.

In the case you described, the officer arrested a suspect in the suspect's car and observed the handle of a gun sticking out from under the seat. The officer was in a location he had a right to be and observed the handle of the gun in plain view. This is a legal search.

In fact, because the suspect was placed under arrest while seated in the car, the officer has a right to search any area under the suspect's control and could have looked under the seat even if the handle of the gun wasn't sticking out.

Any contraband, or in this case, a deadly weapon, could have been seized as a result of the arrest even if it were not in plain view. The key here is to write a detailed, step-by-step report explaining the plain view aspect of the case.

It would also be a good idea to take photographs of the area where the car was parked and of the interior of the car where the gun handle was sticking out.

If it were nighttime, special attention would also be given to the type of lighting outside of the bar and/or whether or not the officer used a flashlight to aid in his vision into the vehicle.

---

7. *What is the first step in the collection of evidence at a crime scene?*

Possible Response:

The first step is recognition of what evidence is. Guns, knives, tire irons and large items such as these are relatively easy to recognize. However, other types of evidence, such as hairs, fibers, semen, blood and fingerprints may be difficult to locate or invisible to the naked eye and have to be enhanced though special lighting or powers.

Because some evidence is microscopic, the type of crime scene and the experience and training of those collecting evidence will determine what's being looked for. Our department has excellent evidence technicians, and my primary job as an investigator is to make certain they have the time and equipment necessary to do their work.

---

8. *A woman was stabbed to death in the basement of an apartment building. You are canvassing the building and knock on the door of a second-floor apartment. A man answers the door and states, "I'm sorry!" His clothes are bloodstained. How would you handle this situation?*

Possible Response:

Taken together, the facts that a woman was stabbed to death, the man has blood on his clothes and he made the statement "I'm sorry" provides enough probable cause to take him into custody. I would advise the man of his Miranda rights, enter the apartment to make certain no other person was in danger, and then post an officer at the front door while I applied for a search and seizure warrant to search the apartment.

Although his apartment is not the scene of the murder and *Mincey v. Arizona* may not apply, there are no exigent circumstances here, so I would apply for a warrant.

I would have to make a decision whether the suspect knowingly and intelligently waived his rights and, if so, I would ask him whether he stabbed the woman. I would seize the man's clothing under the search and seizure warrant to have serology and DNA tests done to see whether either matched the woman's blood. Obviously, I would be searching the apartment for the knife or other weapon used to stab the woman.

Possible Follow-up Question from a Panelist:

How would you handle the crime scene?

> **Note:** Never argue with the oral board. A response such as, "Well, if I were canvassing the apartment, then it probably isn't my case and another detective is handling the crime scene" is inappropriate. Just answer the question. This gives you an opportunity to talk about the importance of securing the scene; what evidence is; the transfer of evidence from victim/scene to a possible suspect; your knowledge of stab wounds; etc.

9. You discover a fingerprint at the scene of a burglary. How would you go about collecting this evidence?

Possible Response:

Our department has specialists who are experts in photographing and using powders and/or chemicals to lift fingerprints impressions and using a variety of data bases to try and match the fingerprint to a suspect. So I would call for an evidence technician to process the evidence found at the scene. Obviously, elimination prints would be taken from those who use the property or home.

Possible Follow-Up Question from a Panelist:

What if no evidence technicians were available to respond to the scene? Would you lift the fingerprints?

Possible Response:

I am not an expert in fingerprinting. If possible, I would properly package the item the fingerprint was on and transport it to the crime lab for processing. If that were not possible, I would wait at the scene until an evidence technician is available either from my city or another agency.

---

10. **There are seven exceptions to the requirement under the Fourth Amendment that the police obtain a search and seizure warrant prior to searching a person, place or thing. Discuss three of the seven exception to the search warrant rule.**

Possible Response:

The seven exceptions are arrest, exigent circumstances, consent, plain view, motor vehicle, inventory and caretaker. I'll discuss arrest, exigent circumstances, and plain view.

The Supreme Court ruled in a 1973 case, *United States v. Robinson*, a lawful custodial arrest establishes the authority to search the arrested person. In am earlier Supreme Court case, *Chimel v. California*, the court ruled that the police may search the area under the immediate control of an arrested person. So if I arrested a person for Breach of Peace and, in a search of that person, subsequently found marijuana in the suspect's pocket, an additional charge could be placed on the person for possession of a controlled substance. If the person had a coat over a chair next to where I arrested him, the coat would be in the person's "immediate control" and I would be able to search the coat prior to allowing him to put it on.

The word **exigent** means "emergency." The key is time and need. If a police officer doesn't have time to get a warrant and there is an immediate risk of harm to the public requiring immediate official action, this is exigent circumstances. If there is a fire in a building and a police officer observes smoke pouring out from under one of the apartment doors, knocks and receives no response, the officer doesn't have to obtain a search warrant to break down the door and rescue an elderly person in a wheelchair.

Another exception to the search warrant requirement is the "plain view doctrine." In 1968, the Supreme Court ruled in *Harris v. United*

States and later in *Horton v. California* that when an officer has a right to be where he or she is, anything an officer observes in plain view is not the product of a search and is admissible as evidence in court. If the police have probable cause to believe something observed is contraband, stolen property, or other evidence of a crime, the police can seize it if they are lawfully in a place and see it.

A classic example is a motor vehicle stop in which the officer observes a gun on the floorboard of the car. The weapon is in plain view, and the officer can seize it without a warrant. If the person in the car does not have a valid permit for the weapon, the officer can then place the person under arrest.

Additional Questions

Ten questions is a lot for an oral board because of time. Depending on the number of candidates, the average oral test lasts about thirty minutes. So six of the ten questions would be typical.

Following are a series of other questions frequently asked on oral examinations. Now it's your turn to construct an appropriate response and practice reciting it.

1. *How does the Mincey rule affect the search of a murder scene for evidence?*

2. *What can be learned from the presence or absence of post-mortem lividity on a body at a crime scene?*

3. *What is rigor mortis, and what can be learned from its presence or absence on a body at a crime scene?*

4. *Explain the Forth Amending particularity requirement of a search and seizure warrant.*

5. *What is a crime scene? Why do we search for evidence at the scene of a crime?*

6. *How is a crime scene properly recorded?*

7. *Discuss the importance of searching for fingerprints at a crime scene.*

8. *What can be learned from blood found at a crime scene?*

9. *What can be learned from semen found at a crime scene?*

10. *What can be learned from hairs and fibers found at a crime scene?*

11. *A woman has been murdered. What can an examination of the woman's body tell an investigator?*

12. *A gun has been found at the scene of a crime. What can be determined from a gun by an investigator?*

13. *Gun powder residue has been found on a murder victim. Discuss gun powder residue and what can be learned by an investigator from its presence or absence on a body or suspect.*

14. *Discuss blood splatter stains and how they may be useful in an investigation.*

15. *How does an investigator estimate the distance a firearm was from a murder victim when he/she was shot to death?*

16. *Explain what DNA is and how it might be collected and used in an investigation.*

17. *A woman has been raped. How will you go about collecting physical evidence of the rape?*

18. *What are tool marks, and how can they be useful in an investigation?*

19. *A partially decomposed body had been found in the woods. Explain the helpfulness of entomology.*

20. *What are the goals of a search of a crime scene?*

Chapter Eleven

Forensics and Technology

It's been almost fifteen years since I retired from the Hartford, Connecticut Police Department and began writing and teaching. One of the benefits of being the director of a college criminal justice program is that I get to spend a great deal of time with today's investigators.

I'm often asked by my students what the difference is between detectives in my era and those of today. Although detective work is still very much a study of human behavior and I remain steadfast in my belief that there is no substitute for years of street-level experience, the most significant difference is the tools available to today's detectives.

The technology and forensic sciences now commonplace have created a shift in the paradigm on how to conduct investigations. It's difficult to argue against the advantages that DNA, forensic fingerprinting and anthropology, and computer technology have provided today's investigator, and there is little doubt that new discoveries will have a significant impact in identifying and prosecuting those who commit crimes.

At the patrol level, vehicles are now equipped with computers that provide instant access to motor vehicle and criminal records, departmental forms and instantaneous information relative to crime patterns. Fax machines in police vehicles are capable of transmitting photographs. Radio communication is state of the art. The formal education level of today's detectives is higher, and they grew up using the type of computer technology that was science fiction to those of my era.

Previous chapters covered some of the uses of science and computer technology in investigating the more serious crimes of murder, rape, robbery, burglary and serious assault. Although information is always good, those of us who teach in criminal justice know policing is a "doing" profession. Knowing about something is quite different from being able to do it.

Because you're not here for me to show you how to do it, the closest we can come to actual "training" is a case study. The case of the parking garage assault highlights the use of modern-day investigative tools while emphasizing the traditional skills of detectives everywhere—to understand human behavior from a psychological needs fulfillment perspective.

In the case study that follows, the lead investigator is a thirty-five-year veteran of the department who is a master of street-level investigative skills and knows little about forensics or technology, but is willing to learn. Also on the case is a detective from the department's evidentiary services division who has a master's degree in forensic science, is working on her doctorate and is a recognized expert in identifying and processing crime scene evidence.

One purpose of the case study is to point out the difficulty departments are having in retaining experienced investigators because of the lucrative inducements offered in the twenty-years-and-out retirement packages. It has been my experience that this case study leads to lively class discussion in either the academic or training arena.

Case Study: The Parking Garage Assault - Part 1

The Assault

Marie Delany is a 32-year-old branch manager of a nationally known bank in Hartford, Conn. The bank is situated in the foyer on the first floor of a multi-level business complex in a heavily industrialized downtown area. Elevators connect the various business offices to a massive five-level parking garage,

On May 27, at approximately 0645 hours, Marie Delaney parked her car on the third level of the garage, walked across the parking lot and took the public elevator down to the first floor to open the bank for business at 0900 hours.

The bank closes at 1800 hours; at approximately 1845 hours Delaney took the same elevator up to the third floor of the garage. Unable to immediately locate her keys, she placed her purse on the hood of the car to search for them. While in this position, she was struck so violently in the back of her head that she fell forward onto the hood of the car, suffering a severe contusion to her forehead over her right eye.

Her assailant pulled her legs out from under her and dragged her backward some 14 feet to the steps of a stairwell. He then dragged her down the stairwell into a small, partially enclosed landing. Displaying a large knife (the back of which he had used to strike Delaney), the assailant forced Delaney to fellate him and subsequently sodomized her. In the process, he repeatedly struck her with the rear of the knife, fracturing her jaw and damaging her right eye so severely it later had to be surgically removed. Her assailant took her purse, told her he knew where she lived and threatened to kill her if she contacted the police.

Some time later, Delaney managed to drag herself up the stairwell. An insurance company employee who worked in the building found her lying next to her car. He called 911, and the police and an ambulance were dispatched to the scene.

The Initial Response

Unfortunately, the insurance employee who found Delaney called the police with a cell phone that provided only partial reception, and the police dispatcher interpreted the call as a sick/cared for. Officer James Jenkins was immediately dispatched (at 1918 hours). But he was across town. When he did arrive in the downtown area, he went to a parking garage directly across the street from the bank's garage. Meanwhile, the ambulance arrived at the correct location and transported Delaney to St. Francis Hospital's critical care unit.

Eventually, Jenkins arrived at the crime scene. He spoke with the insurance company employee, who speculated that Delaney must have been mugged. The insurance employee reported he had attempted to provide first aid by taking off his shirt and applying direct pressure to Delaney's facial area. He said she was partially unconscious and did not speak to him. Officer Jenkins had a little over a year on the job. After noting only a small amount of blood near where the insurance employee reported finding Delaney, the officer left the scene to find out what he could at the hospital.

The ambulance radioed ahead to the emergency room, reporting the severe injury to Delaney's eye. Even with her fractured jaw, Delaney managed to tell the medical response technician (MRT) she had been raped. The paramedics immediately reported the rape to the trauma team that greeted the ambulance at the entrance to the hospital's critical care unit, whose staff was fortunately well-trained in handling rape cases.

When Jenkins arrived at the hospital, he learned of Delaney's critical condition and rape from the MRT who assisted her in the ambulance. Jenkins returned to the parking garage, intending to protect the scene, using his cruiser's radio en-route to call his supervisor, Sergeant Fleming. Because he used his radio rather than a cell phone or land line, every news media outlet with a police scanner marshaled its forces to arrive at the parking garage.

Upon arriving at the scene, Fleming called for more police personnel and sealed off all garage entrances and exits. He used his cell phone to call the detective division. Detectives Anthony Capriati (the Cisco Kid) and Paul Amaral responded to the scene, arriving at 2037 hours, one hour and 19 minutes after the insurance employee called 911.

The Detectives Arrive

The Cisco Kid had been a detective for more than 35 years. His partner, Amaral, had six years on the job, but had been promoted to detective only two weeks before the crime. It was the Kid's case. Amaral's job was to watch and listen.

With the parking garage now sealed off, Capriati felt somewhat confident the crime scene was well protected. He spoke with Jenkins, who was receiving a severe, loud tongue lashing from Fleming. Jenkins pointed out where the insurance employee had found Delaney, and showed the detective the small amount of blood on the cement floor of the garage, along with the insurance employee's wadded-up white shirt. Capriati took out his flashlight, and his eyes moved from the initially observed blood spot to a trail of blood droplets. He followed the intermediate blood-splatter trail and scuff marks to the steps of the stairwell and then down into the partially enclosed landing. What he saw there made him back off and make a call on his cell phone to the home of Detective Shirley Bascomb.

The Evidence Technician

Bascomb was the department's premier evidence technician. Technically, she did not work for the detective bureau, but for the Evidentiary Services (ES) division, which was run out of the patrol division. Capriati had her cell phone number on speed-dial.

Bascomb's husband Paul answered the phone. "Paul, it's Cisco. I need Shirley." Capriati could hear children's laughter in the background and knew he was interrupting a family event. Bascomb came on the line. "I'm in the middle of my son's birthday party here, Cisco. So, whatever it is, call one of the other techs."

"I need you here, Shirley. I've got a woman with a fractured jaw who's probably going to lose an eye. She was raped in a parking-garage stairwell."

There was a long pause. "I'm not on the clock, Cisco. Call somebody else."

Capriati sighed. "I've got blood, a blood-spatter trail, a possible sneaker impression. Maybe some human hair and tissue. You owe me one, and I need you here."

Such a long time went by Capriati thought they'd been disconnected. "Where is it?" Bascomb finally asked.

Capriati knew he had her. "The parking garage, third floor, across from the civic center. Follow the lights on the cop cars."

Capriati made two other quick phone calls and snapped his phone shut. Amaral had heard parts of the conversation. "What do we do know?" he asked.

Capriati looked at him. He liked this kid. "I'll wait for Shirley. You get that rookie cop away from Sergeant Fleming before Fleming kills him and have one of the guys start taking down the license plate numbers of every car in the garage, in the garage across the street, and in a four-block radius. Then go over to the hospital and find out what you can. Detective Lucas will meet you there."

Amaral raised his eyebrows. "Lucas is another crime scene tech. He's on duty right now, right?" Capriati nodded. "But you called Shirley at home and went around Lucas." Capriati nodded again.

There's going to be hell to pay," Amaral said. "Not really," Capriati said. "I cleared it with the boss, and he's on the way in."

"Jetmore's coming in?"

"He always does. Relax. He'll sign the overtime cards and buy coffee."

Bascomb had never wanted to be a cop. She wanted to be a crime scene investigator without the police part. After graduating from high school, she received a bachelor's and master's degree in forensic science from the University of New Haven, one of the country's most prestigious schools in forensics. She was now working on her doctorate. Bascomb soon learned there were few jobs in forensics in Connecticut, and with no way to practice her trade, she joined one of the few departments in the state that offered positions dealing with forensic science. That was nine years ago. She still had to pay her dues, and did her time in patrol, clawed, politicked and tested her way to detective, and finally made it to the ES bureau.

Bascomb arrived on scene in the ES van, which was equipped with everything on earth needed to process a crime scene. "I spoke with Lucas at the hospital, and he's not a happy camper," she said to Capriati.

"So what else is new? He was born unhappy," Capriati replied. Bascomb removed a large, portable light capable of turning night into bright daylight from the crime scene van. "Let's do a walk-through and see what we got," she said.

Bascomb noted the blood on the cement floor of the garage where the insurance employee found the victim and the wadded-up shirt used to provide first aid, and she followed the sporadic blood droplets to the stairwell. She shined the light back and to the right and saw the scuff marks on the ground leading to a 2005 Honda Civic. "Is that the victim's car?" she asked Capriati.

"Yep," he replied. "The plate comes back to her." Bascomb walked over to the car and noted the disturbance to the hood. She shined the light back along the trail of scuff marks. "Looks like this is the place the guy confronted her and dragged her in that direction."

Bascomb followed the trail to the stairwell and went down the nine steps to the landing. She noted the scuff marks on the steps and observed more blood in the landing area. She observed a partial sneaker print in the blood and dirt. The stairwell landing led to another flight of stairs going both up and down, and Bascomb saw faint blood splatters at intervals going down the stairs.. "Looks like she got a piece of the bastard," she said.

She and Capriati followed the blood-spatter trail down the steps to the first-floor landing where they petered out at a door leading outside the garage. Almost simultaneously, they noted a discarded paper soda cup, half-full, with a straw sticking out of the lid. They looked in all directions. They were on the street now, and the rapist could have gone anywhere.

"This is going to take me a long time, Cisco. I have to photograph and videotape all of this, print the car and the stairwell railings, take samples of all of this blood, do a sketch and God knows what else. I need some more help here." She was excited.

"I'll give you a hand," Capriati said.

Bascomb laughed. "You're our best detective, but this isn't what you do. I need another crime tech."

Capraiti took out his cell phone and after a couple of minutes said, "I talked to the boss, and he's arranging for another person from ES to come in on O.T."

"Okay," Bascomb said. "I'll start photographing the scene while I wait for the other tech to show up."

PROFESSORS, INSTRUCTORS, TRAINERS AND READERS STOP HERE !!!

At this point in the case study, there are significant instructional outcomes that you may wish to highlight or engage your students in class discussion about. If you're not attending a specific course, but purchased this book to increase your knowledge and/or skills level, the following questions will increase your understanding of the issues, legal questions, and practitioner obstacles presented in the case study thus far.

1. *Was the crime scene properly protected? How will the fact that Officer Jenkins left the crime scene unprotected, went to the hospital, and then later returned, affect the case? Will evidence subsequently discovered be allowed in court?*

2. *Every police department has a policy and procedure relative to the responsibility of the first arriving officer to protect the crime scene. Is Officer Jenkins's failure to do so a disciplinary issue or a training issue?*

3. *Should the fact that Officer Jenkins left the crime scene and then returned be recorded in official reports?*

4. *An ambulance took the victim to the hospital before the police arrived. Her clothing and person contain vital evidence. Has the chain of custody been broken?*

5. *What can the blood stains, blood-spatter pattern and trail, palm prints and marks on the hood of the victim's car, scuff marks on the garage floor and steps, partial sneaker prints, blood trail leading to the first floor and the discarded soda cup tell us? Can any of it link the rapist to the victim and/or the crime scene?*

6. *How important is crime scene photography? Video recording? A crime-scene sketch?*

7. *What can analysis of rape-kit evidence taken from the victim tell us? Can semen or blood lead to DNA analysis and identify age, sex or race of the rapist?*

Case Study: The Parking Garage Assault - Part 2

At the Hospital

Detective Lucas had a great deal of experience in the forensic aspects of rape investigation, and upon arriving at the hospital was pleased to see that Judy Benson, a nurse trained in rape-case forensic-evidence collection, was assigned to Delaney's case. Delaney's fractured jaw and scheduled surgery to remove her right eye complicated evidence collection. However, Benson was able to get a swab into Delaney's mouth, take an anal smear, secure a sample of her pubic hair and scrape under her fingernails. Benson helped Lucas separate Delaney's clothing and properly package it as evidence for the state forensic crime lab.

Photographs of injuries to rape victims are critical. Delaney was conscious but sedated, and Benson assisted Lucas by positioning Delaney so he could take 35mm photographs and a video recording of Delaney's severe facial injuries and the numerous bruises, abrasions and scrapes to her legs, elbows, arms and lower torso. Benson provided a continuous verbal commentary while Lucas videotaped.

Back at the Crime Scene

Detective Capriati assigned Amaral to find the insurance employee Jenkins had allowed to leave the scene and bring him to the station to give a written statement. Meanwhile, Bascomb had been joined at the scene by another evidence technician, Detective Paul Newcomb, and they were busily processing the crime scene.

Like Lucas at the hospital, they took crime scene photographs and then made a video recording with Bascomb narrating and Newcomb working the camera. They drew a rough crime-scene sketch and also generated a computer-enhanced sketch with laser technology that calculated distances between evidentiary items with scientific precision.

The detectives collected blood at the scene in an eyedropper, and photographed, videotaped and lifted the palm prints from the hood of the victim's car. They labeled and packaged the soda cup and protruding straw as well as the shirt used to provide first aid to the victim. The sneaker print in the blood and dirt in the landing where the rape took place was visible to the eye without enhancement by powders or chemicals. After photographing and videotaping the print, Bascomb decided to take the entire cement block in a 4-foot square to preserve the sneaker impression for lab analysis. This required protecting the print with vinyl plastic while city workers jackhammered the cement block for hours before finally freeing it. Meanwhile, Newcomb worked on the blood-splatter trail.

Across the Street

The Cisco Kid couldn't stand the noise from the jackhammers any longer. He walked down the stairwell to the bottom floor and out the exit to the street, taking the same route as the rapist. He'd assigned patrol units to record license plate numbers in a four-block radius and search for the victim's purse. However, he knew searching trash bins and the like for a purse was a thankless task and wanted to take a crack at it himself.

By now it was almost 2300 hours, but it was Friday night, and the city was alive with the usual bar hoppers, conventioneers, streetwalkers and drug dealers. Capriati stood on the sidewalk and looked both ways on Asylum Street. The street was steeply graded to the right and ran downhill to the left. Directly across the street was the Hartford Civic Center and above it, the parking garage Jenkins had mistakenly responded to.

Capriati tried to think like the rapist. *He'd want to quickly ditch the purse after taking the money and credit cards,* Capriati decided. He looked across the street again to the wide glass double doors marking the side entrance into the civic center, which led to a huge foyer with small shops and food vendors situated in a large semi-circle. He remembered a men's room was directly to the right inside the foyer. Capriati knew where the purse would be while still standing on the sidewalk. He crossed the street.

On the sidewalk by the civic center steps, a hot dog vendor was doing a brisk business from his illegal street cart. Four prostitutes, a civic center security guard and a traffic cop were busy eating hot dogs and laughing. They all stopped when they saw the Cisco Kid crossing the street dressed in his traditional black suit, black shirt, black tie, black shoes and black fedora with a black feather sticking out. Everyone in the city knew the Kid.

Capriati had known the hot dog vendor, Sammy the Snake, for twenty years. Two of the prostitutes were his paid informants, and he'd bailed the other two out of several jams. The security guard was just a kid. When Capriati reached the hot dog stand, he tipped his hat to the ladies, said hello to Sammy the Snake and told the traffic cop to "take a mope."

Capriati addressed the group: "A few hours ago, a woman was raped in the garage across the street, and the guy took out one of her eyes with a knife. I'm going into the civic center to look around the men's room. If anyone has any idea who might have done this, pay me a visit."

"The civic center closed at 10 o'clock," the security guard said.

"I know, but you're going to let me in."

Inside the men's room, Capriati grabbed a couple of paper towels from the dispenser, used them to lift the lid of the metal wastebasket, and saw a black purse with a strap among the trash.

The men's room door opened and in walked "Candy," one of the prostitutes from the hot dog cart. She shrugged. "I drew the short straw. You know a guy that goes by the name of Kong?"

"Sure, but he's in prison," Capriati said.

Candy smiled and moved closer. "Then his twin brother left on a Greyhound Bus for South Carolina a couple of hours ago."

A ripple went though Capriati's body. Byron Jefferson, AKA Kong, was a sadistic rapist he'd sent to prison ten years ago. If he was out, Capriati hadn't done his job. He should have known Kong was once again loose in his city.

Capriati had arrested Byron Jefferson ten years ago after a lengthy investigation into a series of brutal rapes in the city. Jefferson had taken one of the women from Connecticut to Rhode Island, where he raped and left her for dead, but she survived. Jefferson was convicted in federal, not state, court. Capriati was surprised Kong was out of prison so soon.

Capriati called Detective Shirley Bascomb on his cell phone and asked her to walk across the street to process the evidence in the civic center men's room. She passed Candy in the doorway as she entered and raised her eyebrows but didn't say anything to Capriati other than, "Where's your gloves? You didn't touch anything, did you?"

Capriati indicated the trash can. "The purse is in there. He must have gone through the purse, dumped a lot of stuff he didn't want and then tossed the purse in after he was done. Maybe you can get some prints." He told Bascomb he was going after Kong.

Bascomb was worried. "You don't have any probable cause this guy's the perp. It's probably him, but we have nothing linking him to the crime yet."

"He was in federal prison and must be out on probation. If he left the state, that's a probation violation, and I'll grab him for that," Capraiti said.

Bascomb frowned. "You'd better have a piece of paper in your hand if you catch him. We're local cops. It takes a hearing to determine whether a person has violated their probation. You're going to get jammed up."

Capriati laughed. "Nah, I've got you, Shirley, and you're going to call me on my cell phone in a couple of hours and tell me you found me some probable cause. Besides, the blood-spatter trail isn't the victim's. She took a piece out of him, probably his face. He's marked and that's PC."

Bascomb looked depressed. "It would be a miracle if he was stupid enough to leave his prints," she said.

Capriati nodded. "Well, he's not the brightest bulb on the tree. Maybe we'll get lucky."

Bascomb thought to herself that Kong was smart enough to have evaded a task force headed by Capriati and Frank Kelleher, the state's FBI chief, for five months, but she didn't say it.

PROFESSORS, INSTRUCTORS, TRAINERS AND READERS STOP HERE !!!

This situation poses an interesting legal question dealing with the Exclusionary Rule. Remember: The Exclusionary Rule prohibits the government (police) from using illegally obtained evidence against an accused in a criminal case.

1. *If the victim didn't give prior consent for the intrusive collection of evidence from her person, can prosecutors use the evidence in a criminal case against a defendant?*

2. *Can consent be assumed? Can consent given at a later date be retroactive? A hospital employee, not the police, obtained most of the physical evidence. However, the nurse turned the evidence over to Lucas to be sent to the state lab for processing. Is the nurse then operating as an* **agent for the police** *and thus being used to circumvent the Fourth Amendment requirement relative to search and seizure?*

3. *Or is the collection of evidence from the victim an "exigent circumstances" exception to the Fourth Amendment?*

Case Study: The Parking Garage Assault - Part 3

Finding the Suspect

The Greyhound bus station was only two blocks away from the Civic Center. Capriati confirmed that a bus left Hartford at 1945 hours bound for Charlotte, S.C. The first stop was in Atlantic City, N.J., and included a 2-hour layover.

The Cisco Kid left the bus station, got into his car and made several phone calls. Power can be defined as the ability to make a telephone call and galvanize people into action. To people outside the police family, Capriati was just a detective, and a large hierarchy of cops with bars and stars outranked him, but Capriati had spent a lifetime making a significant difference in other people's lives.

He was one of the few people on the job who could get the head of the federal probation department, Steve O'Leary, out of bed to confirm that Jefferson was in fact on probation and would violate his probation by traveling out of state. O'Leary said he'd send an e-mail to the detective division confirming the information.

Only Capriati could call a longtime friend and high-ranking member of the state police to have a helicopter waiting on a pad at the same hospital where Delaney had lost her right eye in surgery. Next, Capriati called Kelleher, and got him out of bed. "Frank, it's Cisco. Saddle up. We have to take a little 'copter ride, and I need your federal jurisdiction. I'll be in your driveway in 20 minutes."

Finally, the Cisco Kid made his most difficult call. He told the chief of the detective bureau he was "in hot pursuit," but it involved a little helicopter ride to Atlantic City with the FBI, and he'd "keep the chief informed."

Modern technology has now equipped most patrol vehicles with a computer, printers and fax machine. Capriati drove his own old car (jet black, of course) at work, so he stopped a patrol officer and obtained several copies of the latest mugs shots of Jefferson to bring along on the trip. He picked up Kelleher, who didn't look too happy, and a short time later they were flying toward the New Jersey turnpike in a state police chopper.

The state police helicopter has a cruising speed of about 100 mph, depending on wind and weather. The two state cops in the chopper told Capriati they'd have to stop and refuel along the way, making it a 2-hour trip to Atlantic City. Since it's a 5-hour ride by bus, Capriati felt confident they would be there long before the bus arrived and have adequate time to come up with a tactical plan to arrest Jefferson.

Both Kelleher and Capriati made calls on the way to Atlantic City, and by the time the chopper set down on the helipad near the Atlantic City Convention Center, a small army of federal, state and local cops were waiting to greet them. It was the local cops the Cisco Kid wanted to talk to. They knew their city, the bus station and the surrounding area.

After a short briefing, they all agreed on a tactical plan Capriati thought would work because of its simplicity. The bus station was essentially a box with four corners, two exits, a ticket counter and restrooms. The plan was for some local tactical-team cops in civilian clothes with duffle bags to act the part of Greyhound bus travelers seated on benches in the terminal. A couple more would wait in the men's room, and another behind the counter in place of the ticket taker. Jefferson and the other passengers would probably make a beeline for the restroom, and they would take him there.

Capriati knew Jefferson smoked; the backup plan was to take him the minute he walked outside to have a cigarette.

After speaking with Capriati, a seasoned Atlantic City detective left the briefing and returned 35 minutes later with a special briefcase for Capriati. The Cisco Kid emerged from the men's room a short time later transformed into an aged woman sipping from some Johnny Walker Red in a brown paper bag.

The disguise served two purposes. First, it broke up the mounting tension natural for cops waiting for the bell to ring, and second, Capriati, who was well known to Jefferson, could serve as a spotter in the bus terminal. The photographs of Jefferson were good, but any margin of error needed to be eliminated in this type of situation.

Capriati's cell phone rang, and the excited voice of Bascomb came on the line. "Cisco, we got him. The fingerprints on the library card with the victim's name on it found in the trash can match Jefferson's!"

Capriati asked, "Are you absolutely certain?"

There was a pause. "Is the Pope Catholic? Of course I'm certain." Bascomb launched into a lecture on "points of comparison" and so on.

Capriati thanked Bascomb, promised her a steak dinner and informed Kelleher.

"Thank God," Kelleher said. "We were on pretty thin ice, you know."

Capriati disagreed, but just smiled though the false teeth of his disguise.

The bus arrived. Jefferson was one of the last passengers to get off. He had a makeshift bandage across his cheek where Delaney had gouged him, but there was no doubt it was him. Capriati stood up from his bench, and seconds later it was all over. Two of the Atlantic City tactical cops had Jefferson on the floor of the terminal before he took two steps. After a brief scuffle, he was cuffed, and the knife he'd used to hit Delaney was found on his person. The Atlantic City cops took Jefferson into custody on a charge of interfering with the police until the more serious charges could be lodged against him in the morning.

Evidence and Conviction

Eyewitness and victim identification in stranger-to-stranger cases often prove unreliable. Delaney could not pick Jefferson out from a group of photographs shown to her. In fact, she picked out another photograph in the display, stating she was "absolutely certain" it was the man who had raped her. Neither the oral nor anal smear contained enough biological material to complete a DNA-typing profile. Although Delaney had gouged a chunk of Jefferson's face out with her fingernails, that also turned out to be a dead end.

Even so, in the end, it was science that killed the beast. The sneaker print found at the scene was consistent with the sneakers Jefferson was wearing. Microscopic examination found human blood on the sneakers of the victim's blood type, which was not the same as Jefferson's. His fingerprint was found on the victim's library card in the trash bin at the civic center.

The coup de grace was the knife and the straw from the soda cup. There was enough biological material on the handle of the knife Jefferson used to repeatedly hit Delaney to link Delaney to Jefferson through DNA-typing, and the straw had enough DNA material to link Jefferson to the scene of the crime. Jefferson was convicted in court and sentenced as a career criminal to life without parole.

The Cisco Kid made his way into the judge's chambers during a break in Jefferson's trial and was able to obtain a *nolle* in a prostitution case against Candy, the prostitute who had given him the lead on Kong.

Capriati, the two state cops who flew the chopper, Amaral, Lucas, Kelleher, Newcomb and Bascomb had the best steaks money could buy, and all toasted to the Cisco Kid.

Answer to the Exclusionary Rule Question

The Fourth Amendment applies only to unreasonable searches and seizures, not reasonable ones. The test is one of reasonableness. Were the officers' actions in gathering evidence from the victim reasonable given the totality of circumstances of this particular case?

The victim is not an accused, nor is she a suspect. Although the procedure for gathering evidence is intrusive, under the exigent circumstances doctrine, it would be reasonable for the police to believe that evidence in and on the person of the victim was about to be destroyed or altered (in this case, during surgery), and a search and seizure warrant isn't required.

Glossary of Terms

Adipocerous A waxy, soapy appearance developing on the body within three months of death, depending on the temperature of the surrounding environment

Arrest (n) The taking of a person into custody for violation of any law, ordinance, regulation or bylaw of the state

Arrest (v) The action of taking a person into custody fro the purpose of charging him or her with a crime

Autopsy Also known as a ***post-mortem examination***, a medical procedure conducted to determine the cause, manner and circumstances of a person's death

Bill of Rights The first ten amendments to the U.S. Constitution

Blood

Serology Testing for blood in a laboratory

Hemident A field a test providing an indicator that blood is present

Drying Time Estimating the time it would take blood to dry depends on the type of surface the blood is found on; the temperature (heat causes blood to dry faster than cold); and humidity (decreases the time it takes blood to dry). Blood tends to dry from the outside toward the middle

Spatter analysis Can help determine what happened by reconstructing where a bloodstain originated and came to rest. Analysis can also determine with a fair degree of accuracy the type and direction of impact that created the bloodstain, numbers of wounds, type of weapon, position of the victim and assailant, and direction of travel

Body, temperature After death, the body cools to the approximate temperature of its surrounding environment. Under normal conditions, the body loses temperature at a rate of about 1.5 degrees Fahrenheit per hour

Bore The diameter of the interior of a firearm barrel between its opposing high sides

Burglary	The unlawful entry of a structure to commit a felony or theft, even though no force is used to gain entry
Caliber	The diameter of a bullet
Cartridge Case	Holds the powder which, when ignited, forces the bullet down the chamber of the weapon and out toward the target
Contact Shots	Made when the muzzle of the firearm is pressed against the body, causing gunpowder, metallic particles, and often, bits of the person's clothing, to be driven inward
Contact Wounds	May result in the shape of the muzzle of the weapon causing an impression in the skin. The gases from the explosion of the weapon are forced into the wound and then back out, causing a bursting effect that often looks star-shaped, with tissue directed outward. Objects at a distance from the muzzle of a firearm receive little or no gunpowder residue
Corpus Delicti	Establishing evidence that a criminal act has in fact occurred
Crime	Defined from a sociological perspective as anything a society says is a crime and for which it punishes
Crime	An act in violation of statutory law (law passed by the state legislature) or an act in violation of federal law (a law passed by Congress)
Crime Scene	All areas in which people connected with a crime—perpetrator, victims, witnesses—moved. This includes the area the participant(s) moved through in order to commit the crime, while committing the crime, and in exiting the scene
Crime Scene, Protecting	Making certain the crime scene is exactly as the criminal left it
Crime Scene Contamination	Adding to or taking away something from the crime scene, altering it so that it is different from the way it was at the time of the crime
Crime Scene Sketch	A drawing of the crime scene to depict the location of evidence and anything else important at the scene of the crime

Criminal Investigation	The process of discovering, collecting, preparing, identifying and presenting evidence to determine what happened and who is responsible
Criminal Investigation	The collection of information and evidence for identifying, apprehending, and convicting suspected offenders—a method of reconstructing the past
Detainment	Stopping or holding a person with "reasonable suspicion" the person has committed or is about to commit a crime
DNA	Abbreviation for Deoxyribonucleic Acid, an organic substance in the nucleus of all living cells that provides the genetic code determining a person's individual characteristics
Elements of a Crime	Specific factors that must occur for an act to be considered a type of crime

Evidence

Circumstantial	Indirect proof from which facts may be drawn
Demonstrative	A demonstration, such as a sketch or drawing of a crime scene
Direct	Either proves or disproves a fact at issue
Material	Whether or not a specific type of evidence will assist in proving an issue raised in court
Real	Any physical object, such as a gun
Testimonial	Evidence in the oral form of a witness, officer or others testifying in court
Weight of	Deals with how "believable" the evidence is to the jury
Exceptions to the Fourth Amendment search warrant rule	Exigent Circumstances, Search Incidental to a Lawful Arrest, Consent, Plain View, Caretaker Function, Impounded Vehicles, and Motor Vehicle
Exigent Circumstances	Emergency: in *Mincey v. Arizona* (1978), the Supreme Court ruled that officers do not have to delay a search if to do so would endanger their lives or the lives of others

Search Incident to Lawful Arrest	In a 1973 Supreme Court Decision (*United States v. Robinson*), the court stated "It is the fact of the lawful arrest which establishes the authority to search, and we hold that in the case of the lawful custodial arrest, a full search of the person is not only an exception to the warrant requirement of the Fourth Amendment, but is also a 'reasonable' search under the Amendment

Consent - Police may search without a search warrant if they have "consent" from a person who has the authority to give it. Probable cause is not required if the consent is "knowingly and intelligently given."

Plain View	In 1968, the Supreme Court ruled in *Harris v. United States* and later in *Horton v. California* (1990) that when an officer has a right to be where he or she is, anything an officer observes in plain view is not the product of a search and is admissible as evidence
Caretaker	Situations in which police officers find lost property, valuables or dangerous items
Inventory - Impounded Vehicles	In 1976, the Supreme Court ruled in *South Dakota v. Opperman* that impounded vehicles may be searched and inventoried using standard police procedures to secure the vehicle and its contents
Motor Vehicle	In 1925, the Supreme Court ruled in *Carroll v. United States* that if there was probable cause for an officer to secure a search warrant, it might not be practical because the vehicle is movable. In a 1981 case (*New York v. Belton*), the court ruled that when a police officer arrests a person in a vehicle, the officer may search the vehicle's passenger compartment, including any open or closed containers. In 1999, the Supreme Court ruled in *Maryland v. Dyson* that a warrantless search of a vehicle may be justified if an officer has probable cause to believe the vehicle contains contraband, controlled substances or criminal evidence
Felony	A crime that may be may be punishable by death or greater than one year in prison plus a fine
Fingerprints	Friction ridge lines are present on a person's fingers, palms and toes. Under a microscope, the ridge lines appear as pores in the skin through which sweat and body oils pass and are deposited on objects touched

AFIS System	The Automated Fingerprint Identification System allows law enforcement to store fingerprints in a database
Latent	When the fingerprint is invisible to the naked eye it is known as a "latent fingerprint"
Patent	When a fingerprint is visible to the naked eye, it's known as a "patent" fingerprint
Points	The individual patterns of the ridge lines that individualize one person from another in fingerprint patterns
Firearms, bullets, cartridge cases	Bullets and cartridge cases go into a separate evidence envelopes or bags
Firearms, evidence collection	Pick up the firearm by the knurled grips or by the edge of the trigger guard. Place the firearm into a properly marked evidence container or affix an evidence tag to the trigger guard
Frisk	A police officer observing unusual conduct and suspecting a crime is about to be committed may "frisk" a suspect's outer clothing for dangerous weapons. A police officer who has a "reasonable and articulable suspicion" that the person stopped may be armed can "pat down" the outer clothing of the person and then, if the officer sees or feels an item he reasonably believes is a weapon, can go beyond the outer clothing and seize the item
Grooves	The low sides of the firearms barrel interior
Gunpowder Residue	When a gun is fired, the ammunition is propelled forward by the explosion of gases created by the ignition of the powder in the cartridge. However, all of the powder is never expended, and partially burned particles of gunpowder and smoke are propelled out of the barrel. Powder is also blown out laterally on revolvers and during the ejection of the cartridge case when an automatic pistol is fired. Objects in close range of the barrel may receive the residue of gunpowder
Homicide	The intentional, but lawful, killing of one person by another
Incise wound	A cutting, or incise, wound is produced by a sharp-edged instrument such as a razor, razor blade, or knife

Integrated Ballistic Information System
Similar to the AFIS system used to store fingerprints, the Integrated Ballistic Information System was developed for use by the Bureau of Alcohol, Tobacco, Firearms and Explosives and contains microscopic images of identifying characteristics found on expended bullets and cartridge casings

Job Task Analysis
A systematic process that defines the exact tasks, knowledge, abilities and performance behaviors requisite to performing a job successfully over a period of time

Lands
The high side of the interior of the firearm barrel

Locard's Principle of Exchange
Dr. Edmund Locard, a French criminologist, posited the theory that whenever people interact with any inanimate or animate object, something is either taken away or left behind

Mens Rea
Latin for "guilty mind"

Misdemeanor
A crime punishable by imprisonment of less than a year

Murder
Intentionally causing the death of another through force, suicide, duress or deception

Neutron Activation Analysis Test
Detects the metal residue (barium and antimony) present when a gun is fired

Particularity
A search warrant must particularly describe the person or place to be searched

Post-Mortem Lividity
When death occurs, the heart stops pumping, the blood stops circulating and gravity forces the blood to the lowest level of the body. This causes discoloration in the lower extremes called "lividity stains," which appear dark blue or purple

Preliminary Investigation
Refers to the actions taken by the first officer(s) to arrive at the scene of a crime

Probable Cause (PC)
Facts and circumstances that would lead a reasonable person to believe that a crime is being, has been, or will be committed. Less than proof, but more than mere suspicion that a crime is being, has been, or will be committed. Rational grounds of suspicion, supported by circumstances sufficiently strong in themselves to warrant a cautious man in believing the accused to be guilty

Rape	Sexual intercourse against a person's will by force or threat of force
Rigor Mortis	The natural stiffening of the body after death caused by the breakdown of amino acids and other chemical changes in muscle tissue
Robbery	Larceny by force or threat of force
Stab Wound	When a knife or similar object is thrust into the body and pulled out (sometimes repeatedly), causing damage to vital organs and /or internal bleeding
Tattooing	When a person is shot at close range (but not in physical contact with the firearm), there is "tattooing" on the skin in the area where the bullet entered the body. It is this distribution of gunpowder particles around the entry wound that provides an assessment by the investigator of the distance the muzzle of the firearm was from the victim
Triangulation	Measuring objects from two fixed reference points and then in a straight line from each reference point to the evidence showing the distance between objects and the dimension of an area
Violation	A crime punishable by a fine and, in some cases, imprisonment

Epilogue

LAW ENFORCEMENT OFFICERS

We

We defend the constitution, freedom, and the American way of life

We willingly step in harms way to protect those who cannot protect themselves

We lead other centered lives-lives which make a significant difference to the people we serve

We are at our best when the people and things around us are at their worst

We give comfort to those whom society is uncomfortable with-the homeless, the helpless, the battered, the weak, the old, the infirm and the oppressed

We give aid and sustenance to the injured

We are a light that little children run smiling and laughing to—those who would steal their innocence cower in our presence

We defend the peoples right to speak and assemble regardless of their viewpoints, the color of their faces, their religion, their ethnic background, or social class

We are the long arm of the law, the defenders of justice, the pure of heart, the protectors of the homeland, the brave men and women ready to spill our blood to uphold our oath of honor

We honor our dead, our traditions, and our creed

We cry alone—lest those who depend on us would lose heart in our suffering

We seek nothing in return for our service—rejecting all who would seek to influence our actions through gift or favor

We are courageous in the face of danger—we never retreat or shirk our duty

We stand alone and bow to no one in the pursuit of justice

We cannot be influenced in the performance of our duty by others who have been put in position of authority or power

We are not a religious order, but like the Texas Rangers of old embrace our calling as a way of life-not a job or a career

We recognize there are no retired or ex-lawmen—only those who are currently active and those waiting for the pipes to call them to duty once again

We know that evil is greatly attracted to the goodness in us and constantly guard against temptation in all its forms

We are the beacons of light, in the darkness created by evil—the light of our shields give comfort to the forlorn and evil can not prevail against it

When We form as a group the downcast are heartened, the outcast are hopeful, the needy rejoice, the old invigorated, and the young sing songs of joy.

We are the true Jedi Nights, the night ranger, subservient to no one, yet humble in the presence of our brothers and sisters.

We recognize that because we have a great capacity for love we have a great capacity for sorrow and are constantly vigilant lest one of us should fall into the grips of despair—the siren call of all who live their lives as care-givers.

We wear the meads and ribbon presented to use by our brothers and sisters only to pay homage to our mentors, teachers, and those who came before us and will come after us.

We accept the insignia of promotion as a special privilege, trembling in fear of letting those down who have put their faith in us.

We reject those who wear the badge and carry the gun, but have fallen to the dark side of pride, greed, temptation, abuse of power, and dishonor.

We treat the disrespectful with respect, the addicted with dignity, the mentally challenged with kindness, and fight evil with good.

We answer the call to service though we may be tired or ill—in snowstorm or desert heat, in natural disaster or national holiday—putting the public's needs ahead of our own wives, husbands, sons and daughters.

We remain physically and mentally fit lest our minds or bodies render us incapable of performing when called to serve others.

We are known by many names—police officer, trooper, marshal, sheriff, agent, inspector, and others. We are different, but yet the same. We all took the blood oath, we all step to the beat of the same drum, we all answer the same call to serve, we all see the unseeable and do the unthinkable.

We are LAW OFFICERS!!!

SON OF THUNDER   DAUGHTER OF LIGHTNING

At sunrise at the gates of heaven St. Peter stood behind the gate to the narrow path leading inside and cast his eyes out among the multitude of newly dead waiting in darkness and silence for his judgment. He raised his mighty right arm and summoned eight angels to hover at his side. "Go among the gathered masses and summon the peacekeepers you find among them," he said to the hovering seraphim.

Immediately the eight angels formed two group of four and flew silently among the crowd that stretched as far as the eye could see. After a time one group of four angels came across a very old man, feeble, bent and broken with time. The angel of death in the form of pneumonia had come to him in the last hours of his life while he wasted away in a nursing home. The second group of four angels hovered over a woman of middle age. The angel of death had taken the form of cancer to ravage her body.

These two people were brought forward through the parting crowd as the angels bowed low before them singing a song of rejoicing: "Blessed be the peacekeepers, they are the sons and daughters of thunder and lightning. Blessed are the keepers of the peace, they are the chosen ones of the most high!!!" they sang.

And it came to pass that in the light cast by the angels the old man and the middle-aged woman were transformed to their former selves. The man was young and vigorous again. He was adorned in the starched blue uniform of a police officer, his shield glowing with its silver light; so, too, the woman, adorned in the uniform of a border patrol agent, her shield flowing forth with gold light. Both walked by St. Peter, heads held high, in dignity and grace. "Come Son of Thunder and Daughter of Lighting, you have earned your place in heaven by your services to humankind!" St. Peter said.

And as the two walked by St. Peter, in unison they snapped him a sharp salute and he said, "Good Job! Good Job!"

A thousand angels began singing, laughing, and yelling, as if in one voice.

"Prepare the banquet! Prepare the banquet! The peacekeepers are here. Rejoice! Rejoice! A son of thunder and a daughter of lightning are among us. Oh, Happy Days! Oh, Happy Days!!"

Then the gates of heaven closed and the warm bright light went out. The remainder of the masses was taken by the darkness of the evil one. On this day none but the two peacemakers were judged worthy.

Many are called, but few are chosen!

Index

Other Titles of Interest
from Looseleaf Law Publications, Inc.

Path of the Warrior, 2ⁿᵈ Edition
An Ethical Guide to Personal & Professional Development in the Field of Criminal Justice
by Larry F. Jetmore, Ph.D.

Police Officer Examination - *Preparation Guide*
by Larry F. Jetmore, Ph.D.

A Practical Career Guide for Criminal Justice Professionals
How to Take Charge of Your Career
by Michael Carpenter and Roger Fulton

The New Dictionary of Legal Terms
by Irving Shapiro

Tactical Attitude
Learn from Powerful Real-Life Experiences
by Phil L. Duran and Dennis Nasci

Condition to Win
Dynamic Techniques for Performance-Oriented Mental Conditioning
by Wes Doss

Advanced Vehicle Stop Tactics
Skills for Today's Survival Conscious Officer
by Michael T. Rayburn

Advanced Patrol Tactics
Skills for Today's Street Cop
by Michael T. Rayburn

How to Really, *Really* Write Those Boring Police Reports
by Kimberly Clark

Building a Successful Law Enforcement Career
Common-Sense Wisdom for the New Officer
by Ryan E. Melsky

Use of Force
Expert Guidance for Decisive Force Response
by Brian A. Kinnaird

Defensive Living – 2nd Edition
Preserving Your Personal Safety Through Awareness, Attitude and Armed Action
by Ed Lovette & Dave Spaulding

Essential Guide to Handguns for Personal Defense and Protection
by Steven R. Rementer and Bruce M. Eimer, Ph.D.

Suicide by Cop
Practical Direction for Recognition, Resolution and Recovery
by Vivian Lord

Police Sergeant Examinations - *Preparation Guide*
by Larry F. Jetmore, Ph.D.

Police Management Examinations - *Preparation Guide*
by Larry F. Jetmore, Ph.D.

The COMPSTAT Paradigm
Management Accountability in Policing, Business and the Public Sector
by Vincent E. Henry, CPP, Ph.D.

The New Age of Police Supervision and Management
A Behavioral Concept
by Michael A. Petrillo & Daniel R. DelBagno

Effective Police Leadership - 2nd Edition
Moving Beyond Management
by Thomas E. Baker, Lt. Col. MP USAR (Ret.)

The Lou Savelli Pocketguides -

Gangs Across America and Their Symbols
Identity Theft - Understanding and Investigation
Guide for the War on Terror
Basic Crime Scene Investigation
Graffiti
Street Drugs Identification
Cop Jokes
Practical Spanish for LEOs

(800) 647-5547   www.LooseleafLaw.com